Challenges

Global learning in a globalised world

edited by Engelbert Thaler

Katharina Einhoff

Global Warming – Earth's Climate at the Tipping Point?

Schöningh

Aspect 3:

Who can save the world? – What political institutions and industry can do (pp. 28–47)

Task 1:
Have a look at the advert, *Eastpak* being a brand name for packs and bags, and do the various tasks on the worksheet.

Worksheet 15, p. 30
Strategy Sheet 16, p. 32
Method Sheet 24, p. 47

Task 2:
The *Kyoto Protocol* is an international agreement to fight global warming. Gather information about the *Kyoto Protocol* (history, targets, measures, positions of different governments) and give a talk to your classmates, who will evaluate your presentation.

Strategy Sheet 13, p. 25
Strategy Sheet 17, p. 33

Task 3:
Renewable energies are considered as solutions to global warming. Study the text *Eye of the storm* written by John Vidal about wind power in Great Britain and complete the various tasks on the worksheet.

Text 18, p. 34
Worksheet 19, p. 36
Strategy Sheet 20, p. 38
Strategy Sheet 21, p. 39

Task 4:
Imagine you are taking part in a demonstration outside the prospective building site of a nuclear power plant that was planned to be built. Prepare banners with catchy slogans revealing what you think of nuclear power and arm yourself with pro or contra arguments.

Worksheet 22, p. 40
Method Sheet 24, p. 47

Task 5:
Read George Bush's speech about climate change to find out about his attitude towards global warming. Sit down on the "hot seat" as Bush's spokesperson for environmental issues and ask the spokesperson any questions you have concerning Bush's global warming policy.

Worksheet 23, p. 43
Method Sheet 24, p. 47

Aspect 4:

Over to you – What you can do (pp. 48–53)

Task 1:
Read the excerpt from the book *The weather makers* written by Tim Flannery (2005) and make a list of the tips he offers to combat global warming.

Worksheet 25, p. 49
Method Sheet 24, p. 47

Task 2:
Carry out a survey to find out how "energy efficient" people are. Present the data you have collected in graphs, charts and tables. Discuss the results.

Worksheet 26, p. 52
Strategy Sheet 10, p. 22

Task 3:
Launch an information campaign about global warming in general but in particular about how everybody can contribute to tackle this problem.

Strategy Sheet 27, p. 53

Task 4:
Imagine you take part in an art project about today's climate and energy policy. Create a "piece of art" for this project and organize an exhibition.

Worksheet 28, p. 53

Aspects of Global Warming

Aspect 1:

Has the end of the world come? (pp. 8–19)

Task 1:
Global warming is increasingly felt in different ways all over the world: catastrophic weather seems to be occurring more frequently, glaciers are retreating, sea levels are rising, … In what way do you personally feel the impact of global warming?

Task 2:
Find out in groups about the different effects of global warming.

Text 1, p. 9
Text 2, p. 10
Text 3, p. 11
Text 4, p. 12
Worksheet 5, p. 13
Method Sheet 7, p. 18
Method Sheet 8, p. 19

Task 3:
Watch the Film *The day after tomorrow* and do the various tasks on the worksheet.

Worksheet 6, p. 15
Method Sheet 8, p. 19

Aspect 2:

Global warming – what is it? (pp. 20–27)

Task 1:
To find out about what global warming is and how it works do the experiment as described on the worksheet.

Worksheet 9, p. 21
Strategy Sheet 10, p. 22

Task 2:
Read the mixed-up paragraphs of the text about global warming carefully and put them in the right order. With the help of this text and the diagram prepare and give a talk on global warming.

Worksheet 11, p. 23
Worksheet 12, p. 24
Strategy Sheet 13, p. 25

Task 3:
Have a look at the different graphs and charts. Choose one and with reference to what you know about global warming explain it to your classmates.

Worksheet 14, p. 26
Strategy Sheet 10, p. 22

Zur Konzeption

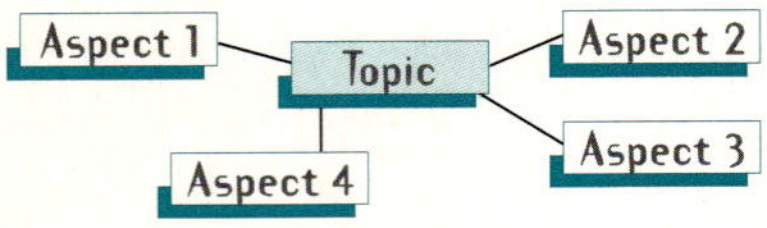

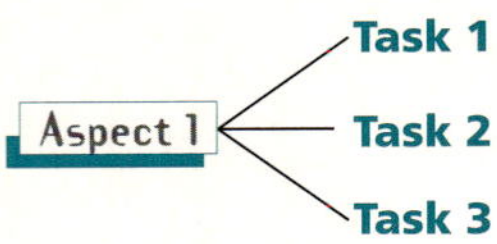

Die Reihe **Challenges – Global learning in a globalised world** stellt zu den 3 Gs des Phänomens Globalisierung (Grundwerte, Gefahren, Gelegenheiten) aktuelle Materialien in Form von Unterrichtsmodellen für den Englischunterricht zusammen. Die Perspektive der praktizierenden Lehrkraft steht dabei im Vordergrund. Deshalb wurde besonderer Wert auf eine übersichtliche Struktur der Hefte gelegt.

- Jedes Thema (**Topic**) gliedert sich in mehrere **Aspects**. Ein Aspect ist in sich abgeschlossen, sodass er auch separat behandelt werden kann.
- Der Lernprozess wird – in Anlehnung an das Konzept des Task-Based Language Learning – durch Aufgaben (**Tasks**) strukturiert. Ein Task ist eine resultatsorientierte Aufgabenstellung mit kommunikativem oder linguistischem Fokus. Aspects und Tasks werden in einer Übersicht zu Beginn auf den **ausklappbaren Seiten 4 und 5** des Heftes dargestellt. Hier kann man sich schnell einen Überblick über den Ablauf des Unterrichts verschaffen.
- Der Einstieg in das Gesamtthema des Heftes erfolgt über eine **Getting started-Aktivität** (Seiten 6 und 7).
- Jeder Aspect beginnt mit **Hinweisen für den Unterricht:** Tipps zur Umsetzung, Alternativen, Bezugsquellen, Tafelbilder.
- Es folgen die **Kopiervorlagen** des Aspects:
  - Arbeitsblätter (Worksheets)
  - Sach-Informationen (Info Sheets)
  - Infos zu Unterrichtsmethoden (Method Sheets)
  - Lern- und Arbeitsstrategien für die Schüler (Strategy Sheets)
  - Texte, Bilder, Grafiken usw. (Texts)
- Jedes Heft wird mit einer **Review**, die Gelerntes nochmals zusammenfasst, abgeschlossen.
- **Klausurvorschläge** am Ende des Heftes erleichtern die Unterrichtsvorbereitung.

Herausgeber:
Prof. Dr. Engelbert Thaler
Autorin des Heftes:
Katharina Einhoff
Fachliche Beratung:
Jürgen Einhoff
Sprachliche Betreuung:
Josephine Einhoff

www.schoeningh-schulbuch.de
Schöningh Verlag, Jühenplatz 1–3, 33098 Paderborn

Druck A $^{5\ 4\ 3\ 2\ 1}$ / Jahr 2011 10 09 08 07
Alle Drucke der Serie A sind im Unterricht parallel verwendbar.
Die letzte Zahl bezeichnet das Jahr dieses Druckes.

Umschlaggestaltung: Ivonne Junge-Illies
Druck und Bindung: AZ Druck und Datentechnik GmbH/Kempten (Allgäu)

ISBN 978-3-14-040201-9

Contents

Getting started

1. Take a look at the cartoon. What does it show? Replace everything you can see with words. Use nouns, verbs and adjectives. Then describe the cartoon to your partner.
What is the message of the cartoon?

2. Answer the questions of the TIME/ABC/Stanford University poll about global warming conducted in the US in 2006.
Find out about what the whole class think of global warming by writing down on a transparency the number of students for each answer.
Sum up the results of the poll in not more than 5 sentences.
Comment on the outcome of the poll in your class. What strikes you as something you didn't expect?
Compare the results of your poll with the results of the poll carried out in the USA in 2006.

3. Write down on a poster all the questions you have concerning the topic "global warming" and pin the poster to the wall as a reminder of everything you want to know about this topic.

4. In the following weeks collect pictures having to do with the topic "global warming".

Poll on global warming

Answer the questions of the following poll about global warming.

1 Has the world's temperature been going up slowly over the past 100 years?

- ☐ Yes
- ☐ No

2 Is the temperature increase caused mostly by things people do, by natural causes or by both equally?

- ☐ Humans
- ☐ Nature
- ☐ Both

3 Do you think most scientists agree with one another about global warming, or do you think there is a lot of disagreement on this issue?

- ☐ Most agree
- ☐ A lot of disagreement

4 Is global warming already a serious problem/a problem for the future?

- ☐ A serious problem
- ☐ A problem for the future
- ☐ Don't know

5 How much do you think can be done to reduce the amount of global warming in the future?

- ☐ A great deal
- ☐ Only a little
- ☐ A good amount
- ☐ Hardly anything

6 Do you think the Government should do more to try deal with global warming?

- ☐ Should do more
- ☐ Should do less
- ☐ Is doing the right amount now

7 Which of the following items do you favour as a way for the government to try to reduce future global warming?

- ☐ Increase taxes on electricity so people use less
- ☐ Increase taxes on gasoline so people use less
- ☐ Give companies tax breaks to build nuclear power plants
- ☐ Give companies tax breaks to develop alternative energy sources

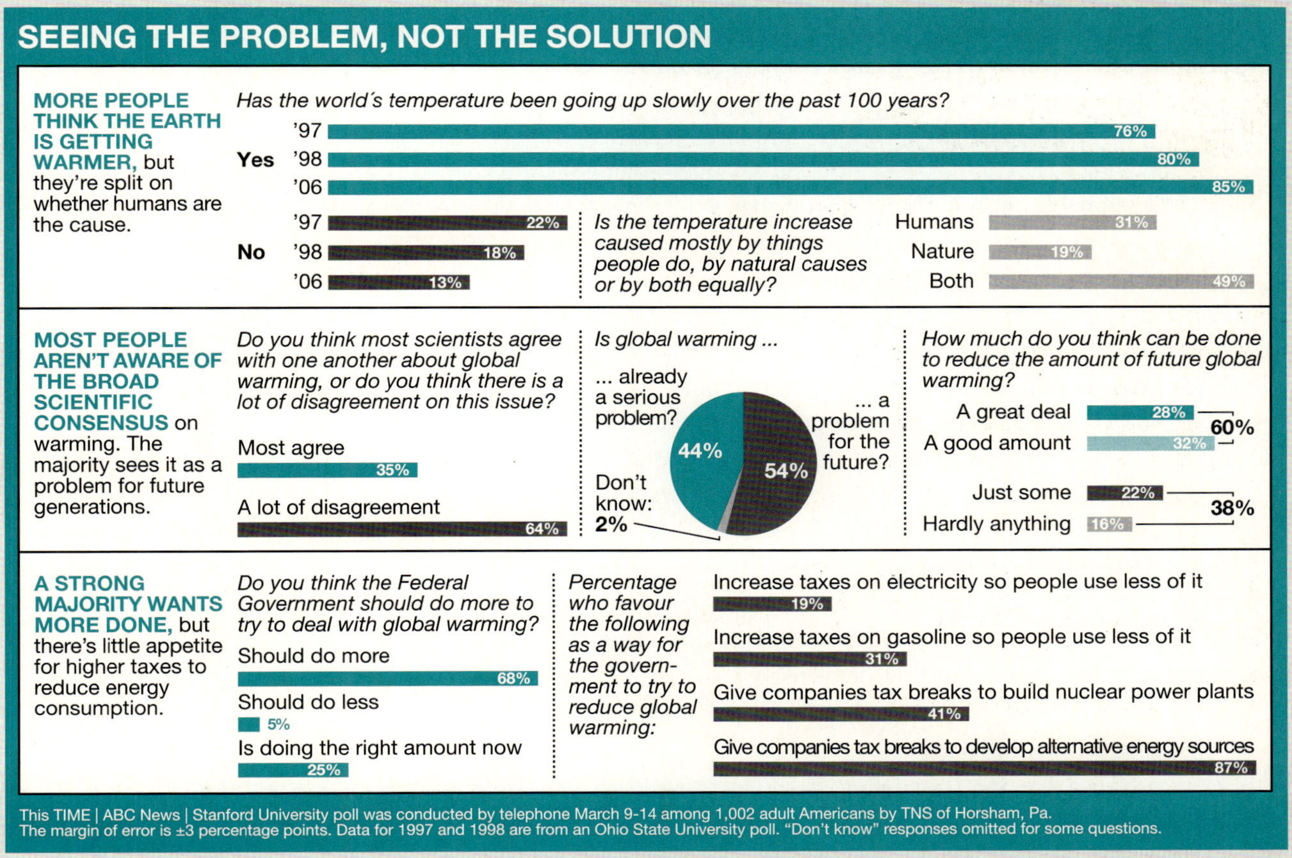

Aspect 1: Has the end of the world come?

Task 1: Global warming is increasingly felt in different ways all over the world: catastrophic weather seems to be occurring more frequently, glaciers are retreating, sea levels are rising, ... In what way do you personally feel the impact of global warming?

Indem sich die Schülerinnen und Schüler zunächst bewusst werden, inwiefern sie selbst von den Auswirkungen einer allgemeinen Klimaerwärmung betroffen sind, werden sie für diese Thematik sensibilisiert und motiviert.

Task 2: Find out in groups about the different effects of global warming.

Mithilfe der Methode des Gruppenpuzzles (vgl. Method Sheet 7, S. 18) werden verschiedene Auswirkungen der globalen Erwärmung erarbeitet. Dafür werden 4 Texte bereitgestellt, die jeweils eine Auswirkung (*weather, polar ice, biodiversity, health*) vertieft behandeln:

Text 1 (S. 9) "Weather": John Vidal, *The planet goes haywire*
Text 2 (S. 10) "Polar ice": *A canary in the coal mine*
Text 3 (S. 11) "Biodiversity": Steve Connor, *How global warming will cause extinction of a million species*
Text 4 (S. 12) "Health": Paul Brown, *Global warming kills 150,000 a year*
Hinweis: Das Worksheet 5 (S. 13), in das die Ergebnisse eingetragen werden, sollte auf DIN A3 hochkopiert werden.

Den Abschluss der Arbeit in den Gruppen bildet eine Diskussion im Plenum mit der Fragestellung:
Taking all the effects of global warming into consideration discuss whether global warming poses a threat to mankind. Are you personally worried about global warming? Explain why or why not.
Alternativ zu einem Meinungsaustausch im Plenum kann die Diskussion auch in Form einer Fishbowl (vgl. Method Sheet 8, S. 19) erfolgen. Ebenso bietet sich die schriftliche Erarbeitung eines Comments an.

Task 3: Watch the Film *The day after tomorrow* and do the various tasks on the worksheet.

Der Film *The day after tomorrow* (Spielzeit 124 Minuten) von Regisseur Roland Emmerich, der 2004 in den Kinos lief, beschreibt die Auswirkungen einer gigantischen Klimakatastrophe.
Dem Klimaforscher Jack Hall zufolge droht der Erde aufgrund der globalen Erwärmung eine neue Eiszeit. Durch das Abschmelzen der Polarkappen drohen Meeresströme zu versiegen, die für die Stabilisierung des Erdklimas verantwortlich sind. Und tatsächlich wird die gesamte Erde von einem gewaltigen Sturm heimgesucht, der die nördliche Halbkugel mit Schnee und Eis bedeckt. Jacks Befürchtungen haben sich schneller bewahrheitet als erwartet. Für weitere Informationen zum Film sei auf folgende Internetseiten verwiesen: www.imdb.com/title/tt0319262, www.thedayaftertomorrow.com, http://de.wikipedia.org/wiki/The_Day_After_Tomorrow.
Die Analyse des Films erfolgt hauptsächlich im Hinblick auf die Auswirkungen der globalen Erwärmung. Ideen für eine weiterführende Bearbeitung werden in dem bei der Stiftung Lesen 2004 herausgegebenen Heft zum Film „The Day After Tomorrow – Ideen für den Unterricht" aufgeführt, das über folgende Adresse bezogen werden kann: Stiftung Lesen, Fischtorplatz 23, 55116 Mainz, Tel. 06131/28890-0, www.StiftungLesen.de.
Als Einstimmung auf den Film äußern die Schülerinnen und Schüler in Form eines Schreibgespräches (vgl. Method Sheet 8, S. 19) ihre ersten Gedanken und Gefühle zu einer Filmszene, die das unter Schnee und Eis versunkene New York zeigt (pre-viewing task). Während die Schüler den Film sehen, erstellen sie ein *Flowchart* aller im Film dargestellten Auswirkungen einer Klimaerwärmung einschließlich ihrer Ursachen (while-viewing task). Diese werden dann bezüglich ihres Realitätsbezuges beurteilt. Abschließend wird die Frage erörtert, inwiefern der Film dazu beitragen kann, das Interesse der Öffentlichkeit für die globale Erwärmung zu wecken (post-viewing task). Die Schüler stellen ihren Standpunkt auf einer „Meinungslinie" dar, dessen Ergebnis gemeinsam diskutiert wird (vgl. Method Sheet 8, S. 19).

Weather – The planet goes haywire

June was cold, the wettest in Britain for 100 years. At one point, it rained non-stop for more than 58 hours in London, the longest downpour ever recorded in the city. The result was severe flooding throughout the south-east. July, too, was miserable and August was "exceedingly cool, wet and windy" with strong gales, storm damage and a rotten harvest. Scotland shivered.

This was not the lost summer of 2004, but of 1903, well before global warming was ever considered as even a minor player in the world's climates.

There will always be freak weather and temperature and rainfall extremes, but what is extraordinary is that very wet summers such as those of 1903 or 2004, as well as intense heatwaves, storms and droughts, are coming thicker and faster as the world heats up. Ten of the past 14 years have been the hottest recorded, and this is linked by scientists to a rapid rise in levels of greenhouse gas concentrations in the atmosphere – which according to ice core samples tested in the Antarctic, are the highest in 440,000 years and still rising.

Almost all climate scientists, atmospheric chemists and oceanographers say the greenhouse effect has arrived and that we should expect more droughts, hurricanes, flash floods, forest fires and giant storms. The kind of extreme weather that happened once in 100 years, they say, could soon take place every 20 years.

There's plenty of evidence that 2004 is falling into this pattern. There have been major fires in southern France, California, Greece, Ireland, Nicaragua and Alaska, where five million acres have been burning. Drought is affecting large areas of east and southern Africa and there have been intense heatwaves in Spain, Portugal, Japan, and Australia.

But 2004 may be remembered for its floods. Just eight months into the year, Bangladesh, and to a lesser extent India and Nepal, have had some of the severest seen in decades, with tens of millions made homeless. Less noticed have been major floods in Hungary, Vietnam, Kenya, Romania, Lagos, Nicaragua, Iran, Siberia, Bosnia and Papua New Guinea. Meanwhile, 17,000 people needed help after huge snowstorms in the Andes and Korea, and there were heavy falls in unlikely countries such as southern Greece, Jordan and Syria.

Last week the European environment agency produced evidence that Europe was warming faster than expected and that the number of natural disasters had more than doubled in the past decade. Last year's pan-European drought cost 20,000 lives and billions of euros and the later floods affected at least 600,000. The agency, which said that most European glaciers were in fast retreat, warned people to expect more flash floods, mudslides, storms and droughts.

Happily, fewer people have died as a result of extreme weather this year. Last year was one of the worst on record, with the Red Cross estimating that up to 700 "natural disasters" claimed 50,000 lives, almost five times as many as in 2002. Heatwaves in India, Bangladesh and Pakistan took temperatures up to 50 C (122 F). In China floods along the Huai and Yangtze rivers swept through 650,000 homes.

The economic cost of extreme weather is soaring. This month's Hurricane Charley caused £ 10bn of damage in the US. Typhoons in China and Taiwan have also caused enormous losses. Last year's losses worldwide topped £ 34bn. [...]

John Vidal, in: The Guardian, August 27, 2004; © Guardian Newspapers Limited

to go haywire to get out of control

exceedingly extremely

gale an extremely strong wind

rotten bad

drought a long rainless period of time

thick and fast quickly and in large quantities

to be in retreat to melt

to soar to rise quickly

Polar ice – A canary in the coal mine

"Climate change in the Arctic is a reality now!" So insists Robert Corell, an oceanographer with the American Meteorological Society. [...] Dr Corell heads a team of some 300 scientists who have spent the past four years investigating the matter in a process known as the Arctic Climate Impact Assessment (ACIA). [...] The ACIA reckons that in recent decades average temperatures have increased almost twice as fast in the Arctic as they have in the rest of the world. [...]

And there is other evidence of warming to bolster the ACIA's case. For example, [their recently issued] report ["Impacts of a Warming Arctic"] documents the widespread melting of glaciers and of sea ice, a trend already making life miserable for the polar bears and seals that depend on that ice. It also notes a shortening of the snow season. The most worrying finding, however, is evidence – still preliminary – that the Greenland ice sheet may be melting faster than previously thought. [...]

Arctic warming may influence the global climate in several ways. One is that huge amounts of methane, a particularly potent greenhouse gas, are stored in the permafrost of the tundra. Although a thaw would allow forests to invade the tundra, which would tend to ameliorate any global warming that is going on (since trees capture carbon dioxide, the greenhouse gas most talked about in the context of climate change), a melting of the permafrost might also lead to a lot of trapped methane being released into the atmosphere, more than offsetting the cooling effects of the new forests.

Another worry is that Arctic warming will influence ocean circulation in ways that are not fully understood. One link in the chain is the salinity of sea water, which is decreasing in the north Atlantic thanks to an increase in glacial meltwaters. Because fresh water and salt water have different densities, this "freshening" of the ocean could change circulation patterns. The most celebrated risk is to the mid-Atlantic Conveyor Belt, a current which brings warm water from the tropics to north-western Europe, and which is responsible for that region's unusually mild winters.

The biggest popular worry, though, is that melting Arctic ice could lead to dramatic rise in sea level. Here, a few caveats are needed. For a start, much of the ice in the Arctic is floating in the sea already. Archimedes's principle shows that the melting of this ice will make no immediate difference to the sea's level, although it would change its albedo. Second, if land ice, such as that covering Greenland, does melt in large quantities, the process will take centuries. And third, although the experts are indeed worried that global warming might cause the oceans to rise, the main way they believe this will happen is by thermal expansion of the water itself.

Nevertheless, there is some cause for nervousness. As the ACIA researchers document, there are signs that the massive Greenland ice sheet might be melting more rapidly than was thought a few years ago. Cracks in the sheet appear to be allowing melt water to trickle to its base, explains Michael Oppenheimer, a climatologist at Princeton University who was not one of the report's authors. That water may act as a lubricant, speeding up the sheet's movement into the sea. If the entire sheet melted, the sea might rise by 6-7 metres. While acknowledging that disintegration this century is still an unlikely outcome, Dr Oppenheimer argues that the evidence of the past few years suggests it is more likely to happen over the next few centuries if the world does not reduce emissions of greenhouse gases. He worries that an accelerating Arctic warming trend may yet push the ice melt beyond an "irreversible on/off switch". [...]

The Economist, November 13, 2004, pp. 89f.

In the past **canaries** were used to detect the presence of dangerous gases underground.

to reckon to think

to bolster to support

preliminary introductory

thaw a period of warmer weather
to ameliorate to make sth better

salinity the concentration of salt in water

caveat *Vorbehalt*

albedo the scientific term for how much sunlight is absorbed by a planet's surface, and how much is reflected

lubricant a greasy substance
to acknowledge to accept that sth is true

to accelerate to start to go faster

Biodiversity – Revealed: how global warming will cause extinction of a million species

A quarter of known land animals and plants, more than a million species, will eventually die out because of the global warming that will take place over the next 50 years, the most important study of its kind has concluded.

International scientists from eight countries have warned that, based even on the most conservative estimates, rising temperatures will trigger a global mass extinction of unprecedented proportions.

They said global warming will set in train a far bigger threat to terrestrial species than previously realised, at least on a par with the already well-documented destruction of natural habitats around the world.

It is the first time such a powerful assessment has been made and its conclusions will shock even those environmentalists accustomed to "worst-case" scenarios. [...]

The study, in the journal *Nature*, investigated 1,103 species of plants, mammals, birds, reptiles, frogs, butterflies and other insects living in six areas – Europe, South Africa, Australia, Brazil, Mexico and Costa Rica.

The scientists calculated the effect of rising temperatures on each species using the three future scenarios proposed by the UN's intergovernmental panel on climate change (IPCC) which has predicted minimum, mid-range and maximum global average temperature increases of between 0.5 C to 3 C by 2050. [...]

A warmer world would push most species towards the poles or higher up mountains but for many this would be impossible. The home territories of those that could move might be so reduced as to make a breeding population unviable.

The study found:

- Of Australia's more than 400 butterfly species, of which nearly 200 are unique to the continent, all but three might not survive in the present home ranges. More than half could be wiped out.
- Brazil's unique savannah grassland the Cerrado faces disaster with some 45 per cent of the endemic plants – some 2,000 species – facing extinction.
- In Europe, the study predicts a 25 per cent extinction rate for birds under the maximum temperature scenario of the IPCC.
- In Mexico's Chihuahuan desert, extinction would be particularly high because threatened species would have to travel long distances to reach cooler climates.
- In South Africa's Cape Floristic region, the scientists believe between 30 and 40 per cent of the Proteaceae, a family of flowering plants that includes South Africa's national flower, the king protea, will die.
- In Costa Rica's Monteverde cloud forests, warmer temperatures would increase the altitude at which clouds form and even prevent their formation.

Lee Hannah, a senior fellow at the Centre for Applied Biodiversity Science at Conservation International in Washington DC, said the combination of habitat loss and global warming would mean that there would be no safe havens even for some of the most-protected species.

"This study makes it clear that climate change is the most significant new threat for extinctions this century," Dr Hannah said. "The combination of increasing habitat loss, already recognised as the largest single threat to species, and climate change, is likely to devastate the ability of species to move and survive."

Steve Connor, in: The Independent, January 1, 2004, p. 1

to trigger to set off
unprecedented sth that has never happened before
to set in train to prepare/ to start with
on a par equal
habitat a place where a particular type of animal/ plant is normally found
assessment evaluation

to breed to reproduce
unviable not capable of surviving

endemic native

Health – Global warming kills 150,000 a year

At least 150,000 people die needlessly each year as a direct result of global warming, three major UN organisations warned yesterday. The belief that the effects of climate change would become apparent in 10, 20 or 50 years time was misplaced, they said in a report. The changes had already brought about a noticeable increase in malnutrition, as well as outbreaks of diarrhoea and malaria, the three "big killers" in the poorest countries of the world. [...]

Diarmid Campbell-Lendrum, a World Health Organisation scientist, said the estimates of deaths were extremely conservative and the reality was probably far higher. They were expected to double in the next 30 years. "People may say that this is a small total compared with the totals who die anyway, but these are needless deaths. We must do our best to take preventative measures," he said.

Although the rises in death and diseases were most marked in poorest states, they were worldwide. Global warming led to drought and a shorter growing season, and malnutrition weakened people, particularly children, making them susceptible to killer diseases.

The most recent example of people being caught unawares was the summer heat wave in Europe, where the initial estimates of excess deaths are still being revised upwards, with 25,482 people now known to have died in the unusually high temperatures, 2,045 of them in England and Wales. In some badly affected countries, such as Germany, the results have still not been made public.

But beside the deaths, there was a large increase in other illnesses. Many children were admitted to hospital in England with kidney problems due to dehydration. Parents and children had failed to realise that they needed to drink more to survive the heat. [...]

The report, produced by the WHO, the UN Environment Programme and the World Meteorological Programme, details how the increased warmth has intensified the spread of diseases. Diarrhoeal diseases spread by bacteria, mostly via unclean water and food, spread and develop more quickly in warmer temperatures and humidity. Dirty water is the largest killer of children under five.

In Lima, Peru, a six-year study at a clinic set up to treat diarrhoeal complaints showed a 12 % increase in cases for every 1 C rise in temperature in cooler months and a 4 % increase in the hotter months. Similar results were found in a survey of 18 Pacific islands. The problem is made worse by high rainfall or drought, where water supplies become contaminated.

Diseases spread by rats and insects are also more common in warmer weather. Malaria, dengue fever and Lyme disease are all on the increase. Many threats can be curtailed by dispensing preventive medicine and providing clean water and sanitation. Climate change makes these issues more urgent, the report said.

The combined effects of increased warmth and the greater volume of standing water brought by storms create malaria epidemics by providing breeding sites and a speeded-up life cycle. In Africa, where the death toll from malaria is highest, mosquitoes carrying the disease are spreading into mountain areas previously too cool for them to thrive.

Paul Brown, in: The Guardian, December 12, 2003; © Guardian Newspapers Limited

malnutrition lacking food or the right type of food

drought a long rainless period of time

susceptible very likely to be affected

excess additional

due to because of

contaminated dirty/ polluted

Lyme disease a disease caused by ticks

to curtail to limit

to dispense to distribute to people

to breed to reproduce

to thrive to flourish

Effects of global warming

Study your text closely. Summarize the effects of global warming and the reasons for the effects as described in the text.

Text 1: WEATHER	Text 2: POLAR ICE	Text 3: BIODIVERSITY	Text 4: HEALTH

Effects of global warming

Text 1: WEATHER	Text 2: POLAR ICE	Text 3: BIODIVERSITY	Text 4: HEALTH
• rapid rise in levels of greenhouse gas concentrations in the atmosphere ⇓ • an increase in extreme weather conditions/natural disasters • extreme rainfalls • flash floods and mudslides • intense heatwaves: ten of the past 14 years have been the hottest recorded • heavy storms: more hurricanes and giant storms • huge snowstorms • severe droughts • forest fires • fast retreat of glaciers ⇓ • increase in number of deaths • rise of economic costs	• unexpectedly fast warming of the Arctic (twice as fast as in the rest of the world) • widespread melting of glaciers and sea ice • fast melting of the Greenland ice sheet • shortening of the snow season • polar bears and seals are threatened • influence of Arctic warming on global climate • release of huge amounts of the greenhouse gas methane into the atmosphere • change of ocean circulation patterns, e.g. of the mid-Atlantic Conveyor Belt ("Gulf stream"), which is responsible for north-western Europe's mild winters • sea-level rise by 6–7 metres	• rising temperatures ⇓ • destruction of natural habitats ⇓ • most species will be forced to move towards the poles or higher up the mountains, which is impossible for many • those that can move their home territories will be too few to survive ⇓ • more than a million species (a quarter of known land animals and plants) will die out • examples: – Australia's butterflies – Brazil's endemic plants living in their unique savannah grassland – Europe's birds – species living in Mexico's Chihuahuan desert – South Africa's flowering plant Proteaceae – Costa Rica's cloud forests	• rising temperatures • droughts • high rainfalls • storms ⇓ • crop losses • unclean food • contaminated water ⇓ • the doubling of deaths in the next 30 years due to … – an increase of malnutrition – outbreaks of diarrhoea – outbreaks of malaria, dengue fever, Lyme disease – a greater number of heat strokes – a rise of kidney problems due to dehydration

The day after tomorrow

1. Have a look at the picture taken from the film *The day after tomorrow*. What comes to your mind? How do you feel? Get together in groups of four and exchange your ideas in written form.

2. Watch the film *The day after tomorrow*. What, according to the film, are the effects of global warming and the reasons for its effects? Draw a flowchart.

3. There is no doubt that *The day after tomorrow* is a fictional disaster movie and not a documentary. Which do you consider to be realistic elements and which just fictional ones? Explain.

4. Do you think that the film *The day after tomorrow* can stir people's interest in global warming? Explain why or why not.

2. ***The day after tomorrow*** **– effects of global warming and reasons for the effects**

global warming

↓

the melting of the poles, e.g. the Larsen B Ice Shelf collapses

↓

the shutdown of the North Atlantic current

↓

a global superstorm

↓

- snow in New Delhi
- huge hailstones falling in Tokyo and along the Californian coast
- devastating hurricanes sweeping over the US
- birds starting migrating south in summer
- tornadoes of unprecedented force wreaking havoc in Los Angeles and Australia
- widespread flooding, particularly along the Eastern coast of the US
- a massive wave (tsunami) flooding Manhattan
- an enormous snow storm covering vast parts of the northern hemisphere with temperatures falling dramatically
- flash-freezing in the eye of the storm, e.g. of helicopters and pilots in Scotland and of sky-scrapers and people in Manhattan

↓

a new ice age

3.

Realistic elements	Fictional elements
• a gradual climate change	• a sudden and abrupt climate change
• the melting of the poles, e.g. the break-up of the Larsen B ice shelf	
• a change in the global circulation of ocean currents involving serious and unpredictable consequences for the world's climate	• the sudden shutdown of the North Atlantic Current leading to a new ice age
• more extreme weather events, e.g. hurricanes, tornadoes and other types of storms	• a global superstorm
• a gradual rise of sea levels, leading to floods	• a massive wave flooding Manhattan
• regional and gradual fall of temperatures	• the sudden and rapid fall of temperatures across Europe and the northern half of the United States
	• the shock-freezing in the eye of the storm
	• a new ice age
• the work and discussions of climatologists	

4.

The film stirs people's interest in global warming because

- it raises awareness for the subject of global warming;
- it gives people an idea of how global warming could affect mankind;
- it makes people talk about the subject.

The film doesn't stir people's interest in global warming because

- people will dismiss it as fiction;
- when watching the film people don't expect to learn anything, but rather want to be entertained;
- people will be waiting for the effects as depicted in the film before they accept that global warming is really happening.

Gruppenpuzzle

Bei dieser Form des Gruppenunterrichts können folgende Phasen unterschieden werden:

1. Erläuterung des Verfahrens
Die Lehrkraft erläutert den Schülerinnen und Schülern den Ablauf des Gruppenpuzzles mithilfe eines Schaubildes (s. unten).

2. Einteilung in Stammgruppen
Die Klasse wird in vier gleich große Gruppen (Stammgruppen) eingeteilt.

3. Verteilung der Expertenaufgaben innerhalb der Stammgruppen
Nach der Vorstellung der zu bearbeitenden Themen entscheidet sich innerhalb der Stammgruppen mindestens ein Schüler für jeweils ein Arbeitsthema.

4. Arbeit in Expertengruppen und Fixierung der Ergebnisse
Die jeweiligen Experten treffen sich in den Expertengruppen, um dort den von ihnen ausgewählten Arbeitsbereich gemeinsam zu bearbeiten. Die verschiedenen Texte werden unter der vorgegebenen Aufgabenstellung gelesen, Fragen werden geklärt und die Arbeitsergebnisse werden gemeinsam stichpunktartig in das vorgegebene Arbeitsblatt eingetragen.

5. Bericht der Experten in den Stammgruppen
Die Experten kehren in ihre Stammgruppen zurück und berichten dort wechselseitig über ihre Arbeitsergebnisse, d. h. jeder Schüler ist jeweils einmal Berichterstatter und dreimal Zuhörer. Jeder Schüler notiert die Ergebnisse der anderen Expertengruppen auf dem vorgegebenen Arbeitsblatt. Hierbei ist darauf zu achten, dass die Schüler die Ergebnisse der Experten nicht einfach kopieren, sondern sich die vorgetragenen Erläuterungen der Experten zunächst anhören, um sich anschließend Notizen zu machen.

6. Zusammenfassung
Die zusammenfassende Betrachtung der Ergebnisse aller Gruppen erfolgt über eine Diskussion.

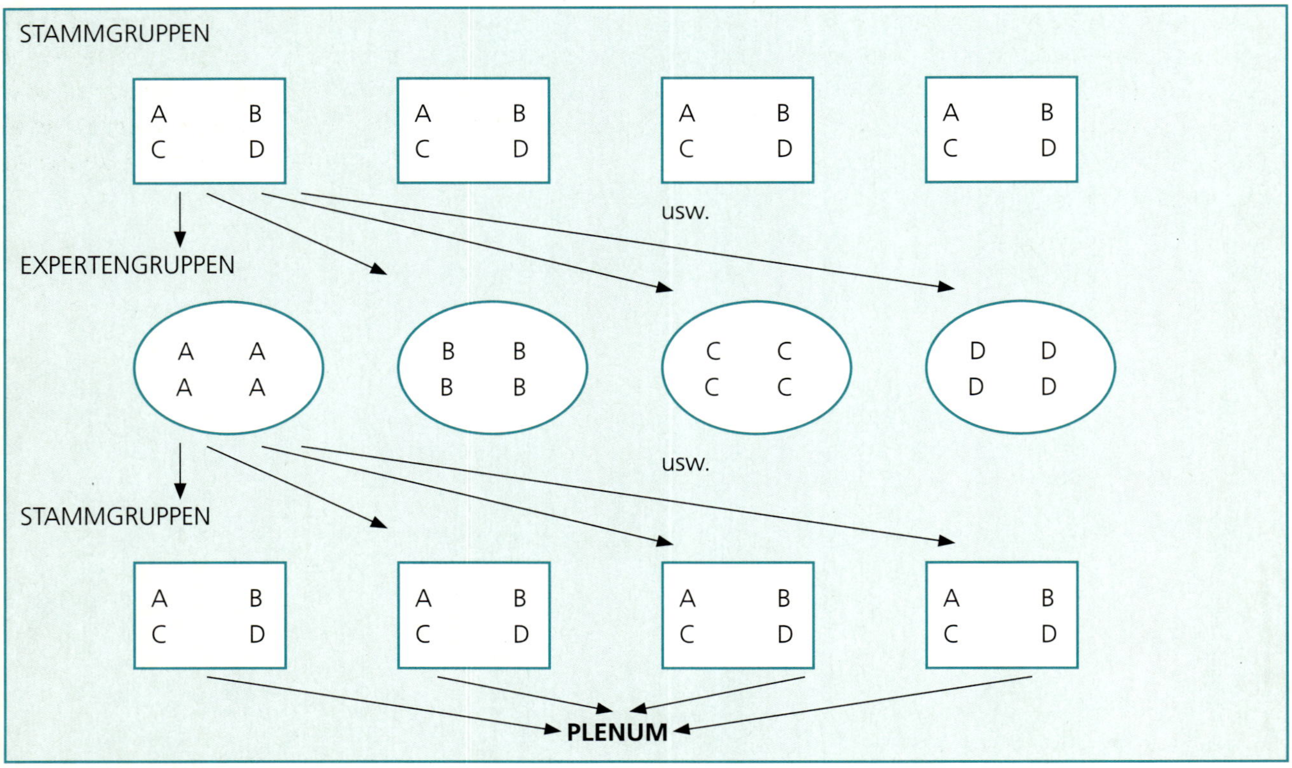

Fishbowl

Die hier vorgestellte Vorgehensweise für eine Fishbowl-Diskussion stellt nur eine Variante dieser Methode dar. Gleich einem Aquarium sitzt eine Gruppe von vier bis acht Schülerinnen und Schülern in einem Innenkreis und diskutiert eine vorgegebene Fragestellung, während alle anderen Schüler die Diskussion von außen aufmerksam verfolgen. Um zu gewährleisten, dass dies auch geschieht, erhält jeder Schüler eine Anzahl von Karten, die er am Ende der Diskussion einem Moderator abgegeben haben muss. Eine Karte kann durch einen Redebeitrag im diskutierenden Innenkreis eingelöst werden. Hierzu setzt sich der Schüler auf einen bereitstehenden freien Stuhl im Innenkreis. Sobald der freie Stuhl des Innenkreises besetzt ist, darf sich ein anderer Schüler der Diskussionsrunde zurückziehen und in die Beobachterrolle schlüpfen.

Schreibgespräch

Ein vorgegebener Impuls (z. B. einer Frage, eine provokative Aussage, ein unvollständiger Satz, ein Bild) wird in einer Gruppe von vier Schülerinnen und Schülern in schriftlicher Form diskutiert. Es entwickelt sich ein Schreibgespräch. Jeder Schüler schreibt zunächst seine Gedanken zu dem Impuls auf. Anschließend wird das Blatt an einen Mitschüler oder eine Mitschülerin der Gruppe weitergereicht, der oder die das Geschriebene schriftlich kommentiert. Wenn gewünscht, wird das Blatt wiederum weitergereicht, so dass der nächste Schüler die Beiträge seiner Mitschüler reflektiert. Abschließend sollten einzelne Schreibgespräche vor dem Plenum zusammenfassend dargestellt werden.

Meinungslinie

Die Schüler beziehen auf einer imaginären oder auf einer mit Kreppband auf den Boden geklebten Linie Position zu einer Fragestellung mit zwei klaren Polen. Bei der hier vorliegenden Fragestellung können die Schüler zwischen den Polen „The film stirs a great amount of interest in people for global warming" und „The film doesn't stir people's interest at all for global warming" wählen. Dabei können die Unentschiedenen auch eine Position zwischen den Polen einnehmen. Das entstandene Bild wird zunächst zusammengefasst und gedeutet, bevor der Lehrer einzelne Schüler auffordert, ihre Position zu erläutern.

Aspect 2: Global warming – what is it?

Task 1: To find out about what global warming is and how it works do the experiment as described on the worksheet.

Anhand eines Experiments (Worksheet 9, S. 21), das gemeinsam in der Schule oder als Hausaufgabe durchgeführt wird, wird den Schülerinnen und Schülern der Treibhauseffekt, der der globalen Erderwärmung zugrunde liegt, eindrücklich veranschaulicht. Die Beobachtungen werden in einer Tabelle festgehalten und als Kurve dargestellt. Die Ergebnisse werden beschrieben und ausgewertet (Strategy Sheet 10, S. 22).

Task 2: Read the mixed-up paragraphs of the text about global warming carefully and put them in the right order. With the help of this text and the diagram prepare and give a talk on global warming.

Ausgangspunkt für diese Aufgabe ist ein informativer Text (Worksheet 11, S. 23), der den Vorgang der globalen Erderwärmung näher erläutert, wobei zunächst der natürliche Prozess beschrieben wird, um dann auf die Ursachen für eine offensichtliche Störung dieses Prozesses einzugehen. Um ein genaues Verständnis des Textes sicherzustellen, bringen die Schülerinnen und Schüler zunächst die verschiedenen Teile des Textpuzzles in die richtige Reihenfolge.
Hinweis: Die hellgrau gedruckten Zahlen auf Worksheet 11 sollten getilgt werden oder der Kopierer sollte bei der Vervielfältigung auf hell eingestellt werden.
Mithilfe der Informationen aus dem Text bereiten die Schüler nun einen „wissenschaftlich" ausgerichteten Vortrag über die globale Erderwärmung vor (Strategy Sheet 13, S. 25). Dabei wälzen sie den eher trockenen Text sprachlich und inhaltlich um. Zur Veranschaulichung dient ihnen das Schaubild „The greenhouse effect" (Worksheet 12, S. 24).

Task 3: Have a look at the different graphs and charts. Choose one and with reference to what you know about global warming explain it to your classmates.

Aufbauend auf ihrem Wissen über die globale Erwärmung, werten die Schülerinnen und Schüler nun verschiedene Diagramme aus (Worksheet 14, S. 26f. und Strategy Sheet 10, S. 22).

Global warming – an experiment

What is global warming and how does it work?

Materials needed

- 2 cardboard boxes of the same kind
- black paper
- 1 or 2 thermometers
- clear plastic wrap or a pane of glass
- (2 lamps with a 100-watt bulb)

Procedure

- Line the inside of the two boxes with black paper.
- Cover one of the boxes with clear plastic wrap or a pane of glass.
- Place the boxes in the sun (or under a lamp).
- Measure the temperature in the boxes every 3 to 5 minutes and jot down the temperature in the table below.

Time	Temperature box 1	Temperature box 2

1. Create a graph of the data of your experiment.

2. Describe and analyse the results of the experiment.
The effect you have been able to observe is called the "greenhouse effect". A similar effect contributes to the warming of the earth.

How to work with graphs, charts and tables

When looking at graphs, charts and tables you can ask the following questions:

- What is the graph, chart or table about?
- What do the numbers of the graph, chart or table represent?
- Check the numbers for high/low points and for trends.
- What conclusions can be drawn from the graph, chart or table as a whole?

Useful phrases

The graph/chart/table …
- gives information about …
- illustrates/shows/proves/indicates that …
- shows the development of …

It draws attention to the fact that …

The numbers represent/stand for/show …

Ten per cent of …
The number/percentage/quantity of … is high/low/negligible …
The number/percentage/quantity of …
- has increased/risen/gone up/climbed up (to/by) …
- has decreased/fallen/gone down/dropped/declined (to/by) …
- has remained stable/constant since 2000.
- reached its peak in 2006.

There is/was/has been
- an increase in …
- a growth in/of …
- a decline in/of …
- a decrease in/of …
- a reduction in …

Compared with/to …
In comparison with …
The number/percentage/quantity of …
- is similar to …
- is identical to …
- is different from …

Twice/Three times/Four times as many as …
Half of/One third of …
An overwhelming majority …
Only a minority …

dramatically
drastic/drastically
huge(ly)/enormous(ly)
substantial(ly)/significant(ly)
considerable/considerably
moderate(ly)
slight(ly)/a little
constant(ly)/steady/steadily
sudden(ly)/abrupt(ly)
fast
slow(ly)

Global warming

4 With temperatures having increased 0.6 +/- 0.2 C since the late 19th century this natural greenhouse effect seems to be out of balance. Scientists even expect the average global surface temperature to rise 0.6 – 2.5 C in the next fifty years, and 1.4 – 5.8 C in the next century.

6 Why is the amount of greenhouse gas increasing? Many scientists are convinced that the burning of fossil fuels (e.g. oil, coal, natural gas), cement manufacture, deforestation and agriculture and other human activities have added and will add large amounts of greenhouse gases to the atmosphere.
The concentration of carbon dioxide, for example, one of the main greenhouse gases, has been building up in the atmosphere at an alarming rate – it has risen by about 30 % – since the Industrial Revolution about 200 years ago, when humans started to use fossil fuels as a cheap energy source.

2 When sunlight enters the earth's atmosphere, most of the sun's radiation is absorbed by the earth's surface, warming it. To keep the earth cool, some heat is emitted by the earth's surface back into space in the form of infrared radiation.

9 Not only the rising level of greenhouse gases but the increase of tiny particles in the air, the so-called aerosols, are believed to have a significant effect on our climate, too. By reflecting the sunlight, they have a cooling effect, thereby partly offsetting global warming.

3 Some of the infrared radiation passes through the atmosphere, but some is absorbed and re-emitted by the greenhouse gases, contributing to the warming of the earth's surface. This warming is called "greenhouse effect", although strictly speaking the term is not applied correctly, because in a real greenhouse heat is literally trapped by glass and not absorbed and re-emitted. Without the greenhouse effect the earth's average temperature would be about 30 C lower. Our planet would be a frozen and desolate place.

10 To forecast the development of future greenhouse gas emissions and their effect on the earth's temperature is difficult, as it depends on the future development of the population, the economy, technology and key international institutions.

7 Other natural greenhouse gases such as methane and nitrous oxide have also been increasing. In fact, the amount of methane has even doubled since the Industrial Revolution, with rice fields, domestic animals, and coal mining being the main sources. Nitrous oxide is released for example when farmers use nitrogen-based fertilizers to get higher crop yields.

1 The earth is covered by a thin layer of mixed gases called the atmosphere. It consists of about 79 % nitrogen, 20 % oxygen and contains traces of different gases, e.g. carbon dioxide, water vapour, methane, nitrous oxide. These gases are referred to as greenhouse gases.

8 Apart from the natural greenhouse gases entirely human-made gases such as CFCs (chlorofluorocarbons) add to the warming of the earth, too. They are used as refrigerants in refrigerators and air conditioners, for example. As their production has been regulated by international agreements to protect the earth's ozone layer their amount in the atmosphere has declined and will decrease further.

5 Scientists generally believe that the primary source of this temperature rise of the earth is the increasing amount of carbon dioxide and other greenhouse gases enhancing the ability of the earth's atmosphere to trap heat.

Katharina Einhoff

The greenhouse effect

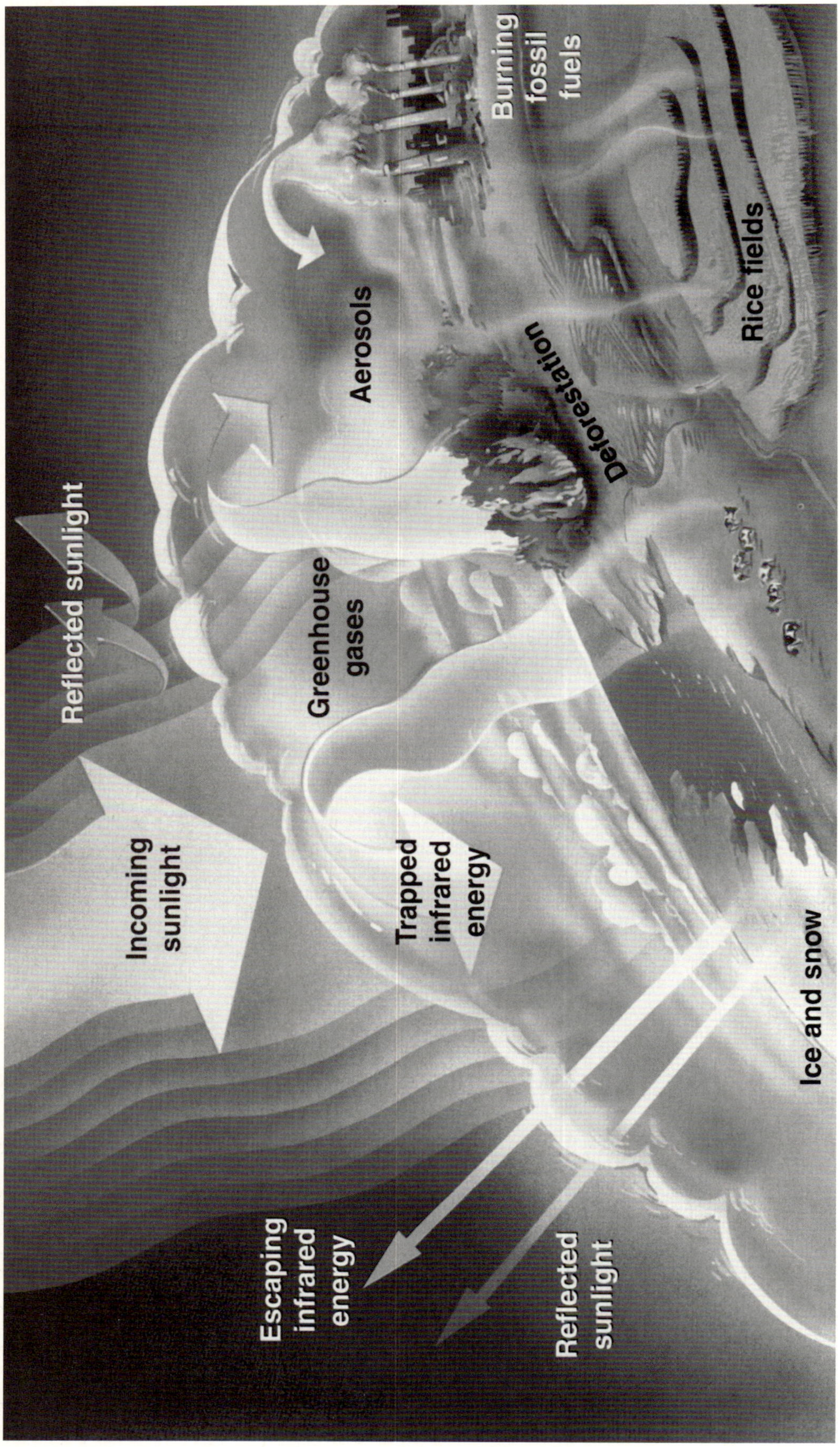

How to give a presentation

Preparing a presentation

- Gather information about your subject.
- Choose the information you want to include in your presentation. The information should be clear, concise, interesting and up-to-date. Keep in mind how much time you have got to present your subject.
- Organize your information giving it a clear and logical structure.
- Prepare prompt cards, on which you write key words or key phrases as reminders of what you want to say. Only use one side of the card and write clearly. Number your prompt cards according to the structure of your presentation.
- Think about how you want to connect your ideas.
- Think of ways to visualize the information you want to convey. Overhead transparencies, computer slide shows (e.g. *Powerpoint*) or posters can serve as visual aids.
- Make sure the technical equipment you need is available and you know how to handle it.
- Decide whether you want to prepare a handout for your audience.
- Check the pronunciation of difficult words.
- Be prepared to explain unknown or difficult words to your audience.
- Rehearse your presentation. You can do this either in front of a mirror or in front of friends.

Giving a presentation

- First, greet your audience and introduce yourself.
- If possible, begin with a challenging statement, a joke, a "special effect", an object or something else to catch the audience's attention.
- Introduce and explain your topic and outline the points you intend to cover during your talk.
- Say whether you will accept questions during your talk or whether you rather want your audience to wait until the end.
- With the help of your prompt cards talk about your subject. Do not read your notes, but speak freely.
- Keep your sentences short and your language simple.
- Speak clearly, loudly and slowly so that everybody can follow what you have got to say.
- Make sure you talk to the audience.
- Use a pointer when employing visual aids.
- Take care not to stick to one place, on the other hand don't move around too much. Use calm gestures to underline your points.
- Finally, draw a conclusion by summarizing the most important points of your talk. Thank your audience for their attention. Invite them to ask questions.

Useful phrases

Let me introduce myself.
The topic of my presentation is …/I'm going to talk about …
First of all I would like to give you an outline of my talk. It consists of x parts.
First I'll …/Second I'll…/Then I'll go on to … After that I'll … And finally I'll say something about …
If you have any questions, don't hesitate to interrupt me./I'll be happy to answer any questions at the end of my talk.
To start with I would like to …/I'd like to begin with …
Now I would like to look at/take a closer look at …
That's all I have to say about …
Now that I … I would like to move on/turn to …
That brings me to the next point./The next important point is … /A further interesting aspect of this is …
Finally I want to draw your attention to …
In conclusion, I'd like to say …/To conclude, I'd like to …/Finally, …/To sum up, …
I would like to thank you very much for your attention.

①
CHANGES IN GLOBAL TEMPERATURE

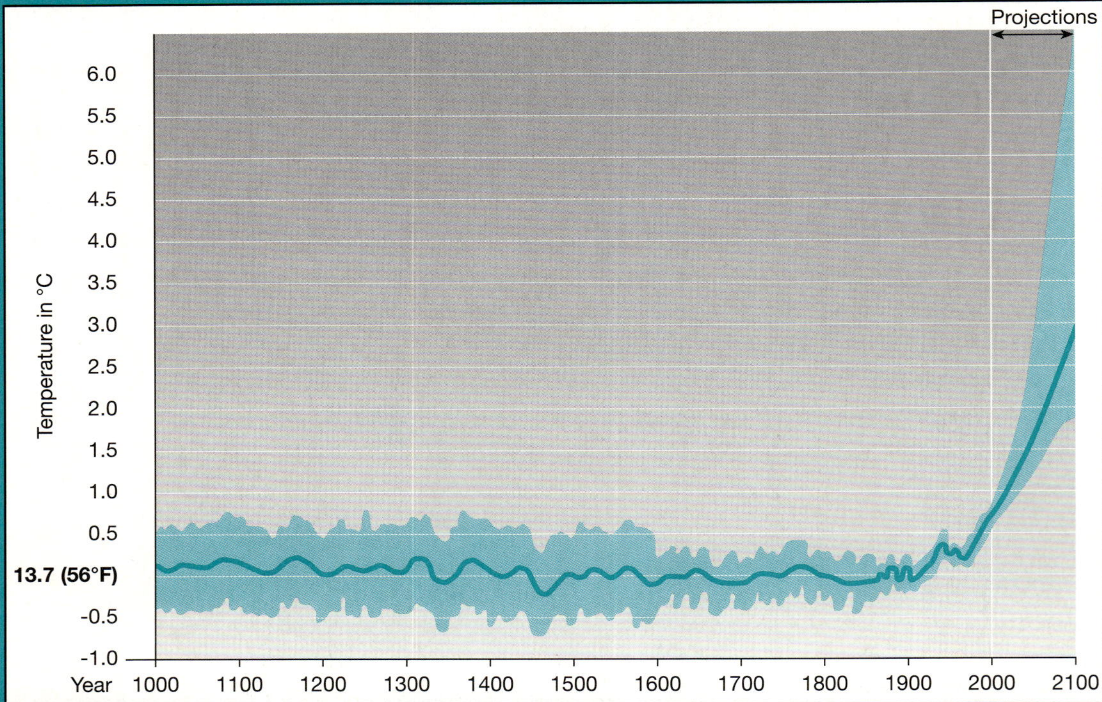

Data: Tim Flannery, *The Weather Makers*, Melbourne, Text Publishing Company, 2005, p. 163

②
GLOBAL ATMOSPHERIC CONCENTRATION OF CO_2

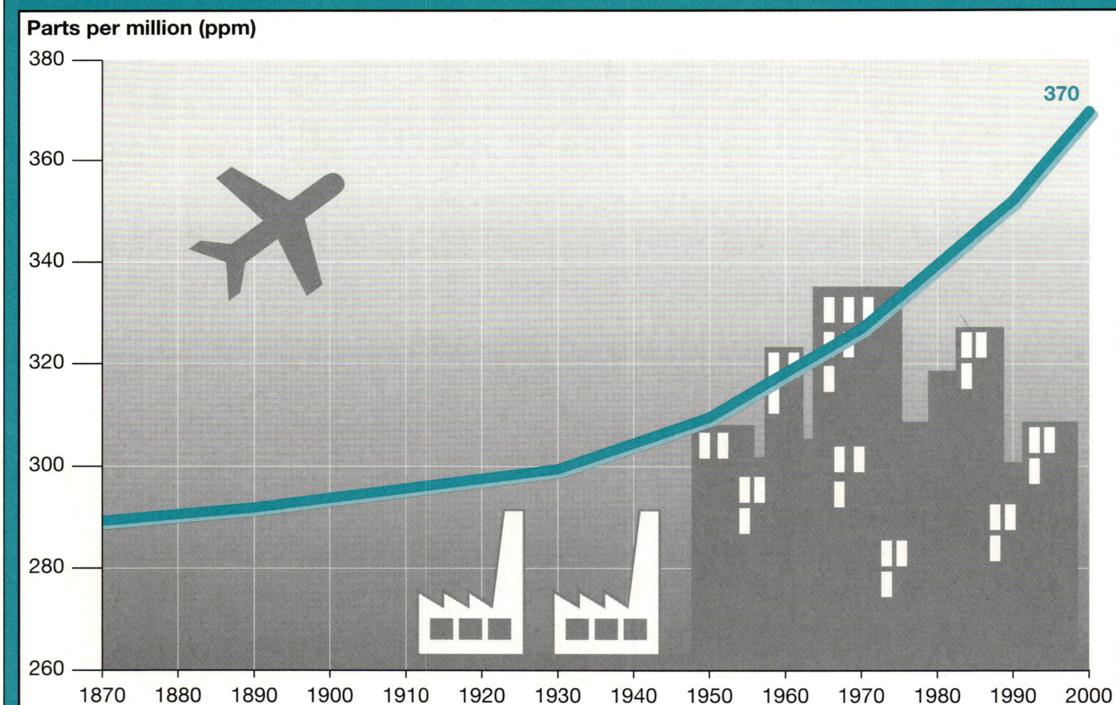

Data: TP Whorf Scipps, Mauna Loa Observatory, Hawaii, Institution of oceanography (SIO), University of California La Jolla, California, United States, 1999

③

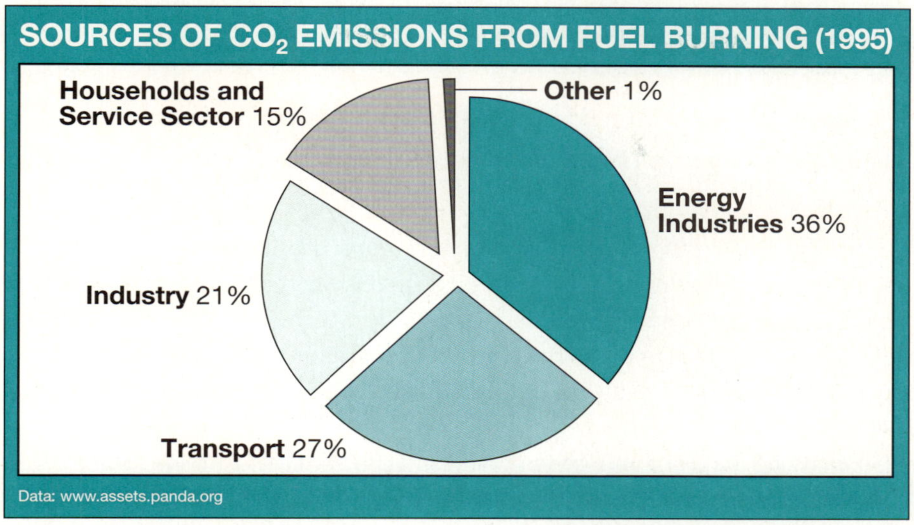
SOURCES OF CO2 EMISSIONS FROM FUEL BURNING (1995)
Households and Service Sector 15%
Other 1%
Energy Industries 36%
Industry 21%
Transport 27%
Data: www.assets.panda.org

④

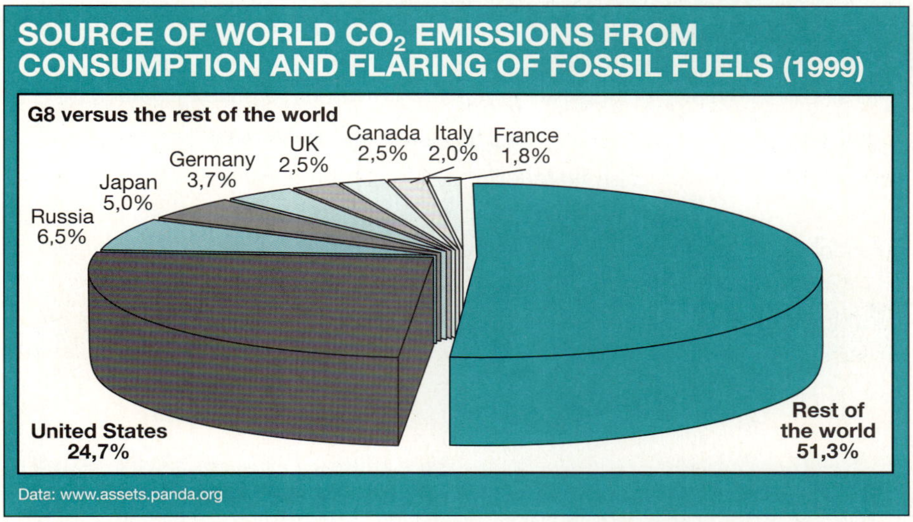
SOURCE OF WORLD CO2 EMISSIONS FROM CONSUMPTION AND FLARING OF FOSSIL FUELS (1999)
G8 versus the rest of the world
Russia 6,5%
Japan 5,0%
Germany 3,7%
UK 2,5%
Canada 2,5%
Italy 2,0%
France 1,8%
United States 24,7%
Rest of the world 51,3%
Data: www.assets.panda.org

Aspect 3: Who can save the world? – What political institutions and industry can do

Task 1: Have a look at the advert, *Eastpak* being a brand name for packs and bags, and do the various tasks on the worksheet.

Die Beschreibung der Anzeige (Worksheet 15, S. 30) erfolgt in Partnerarbeit, wobei das Bild nur einem Schüler vorliegt, der dieses seinem Partner so beschreibt, dass er es nachzeichnen kann. Hilfestellungen dafür finden sich auf Strategy Sheet 16, S. 32. Die Anzeige könnte über OHF präsentiert werden. Während der beschreibende Schüler das Bild sehen kann, setzt sich der zeichnende Schüler so hin, dass er das Bild nicht sieht. Der Werbespruch wird abgedeckt. Der Vergleich der angefertigten Zeichnung mit dem Original zeigt, wie gut das Bild beschrieben bzw. wie gut die Beschreibung in der Zeichnung umgesetzt wurde.
Im Anschluss kreieren die Schülerinnen und Schüler ihre eigenen Werbesprüche zu dieser Anzeige, bevor sie diese in ihrer Gesamtheit nach dem AIDA-Prinzip analysieren (Strategy Sheet 16, S. 32). Die abschließend selbst entworfenen Anzeigen werden im Rahmen einer Pyramidendiskussion bewertet (vgl. Method Sheet 24, S. 47). Die einzelnen Bewertungen müssen jeweils begründet werden.

Task 2: The *Kyoto Protocol* is an international agreement to fight global warming. Gather information about the *Kyoto Protocol* (history, targets, measures, positions of different governments) and give a talk to your classmates, who will evaluate your presentation.

Mithilfe des Internets holen die Schülerinnen und Schüler in Einzel-, Partner- oder Gruppenarbeit Informationen zum Kyoto Protokoll ein, wobei die o. a. Aspekte den Schülern helfen, die vielfältigen Informationen zu strukturieren. Anschließend werden die Informationen den Mitschülern in Form eines Vortrags vorgestellt (vgl. Strategy Sheet 13, S. 25). Um einerseits den Rednern ein Feedback zu geben und um andererseits ein aktives Zuhören der Mitschüler sicherzustellen, werden die Vorträge von letzteren evaluiert (Strategy Sheet 17, S. 33).
Informationen können u. a. unter folgenden Internetadressen eingeholt werden:

- www.wikipedia.org
- unfccc.int/2860.php
- www.greenpeace.org
- www.wwf.org
- www.foe.org

Hinweis: Das Strategy Sheet 17 (S. 33), in das Kommentare eingetragen werden, sollte auf DIN A3 hochkopiert werden.

Task 3: Renewable energies are considered as solutions to global warming. Study the text *Eye of the storm* written by John Vidal about wind power in Great Britain and complete the various tasks on the worksheet.

Der Text *Eye of the storm* von John Vidal wird anhand von Worksheet 19 (S. 36) bearbeitet. In Vorbereitung auf die folgenden Texte und Aufgaben werden zunächst anhand einer Karikatur (Worksheet 19, S. 36) in Form eines Brainstorming derzeit diskutierte Möglichkeiten der Bekämpfung der globalen Erwärmung gesammelt, wobei der Lehrer den Schülerinnen und Schülern die Karikatur so präsentiert, dass die abgebildeten „Lösungen" (Windenergie und Kernenergie) zunächst verdeckt sind. Die von den Schülern genannten Lösungsmöglichkeiten werden auf der Karikatur notiert, um im Anschluss daran die in der Karikatur angesprochenen Lösungen näher zu betrachten.
Anschließend holen die Schüler Informationen über die Situation der Windenergietechnologie in Deutschland ein und vergleichen sie mit der in Text 18 (S. 34) beschriebenen Situation in Großbritannien. Die aus dem Text herausgearbeiteten Pro- und Contraargumente werden in Form einer Gemeinderatssitzung umgewälzt (Strategy Sheet 20, S. 38). Das Ver-

fassen eines Newspaper reports über die Gemeinderatssitzung stellt eine Vertiefung in schriftlicher Form dar (Strategy Sheet 21, S. 39).
Über den Text hinaus informieren sich die Schüler über weitere Formen von erneuerbaren Energien. Hierzu beschäftigt sich jeder Schüler als Experte mit einer Form der Energiegewinnung. Die Präsentation erfolgt in kleinen Gruppen, in denen sich die Experten jeweils gegenseitig über ihr Thema informieren.

Task 4: Imagine you are taking part in a demonstration outside the prospective building site of a nuclear power plant that was planned to be built. Prepare banners with catchy slogans revealing what you think of nuclear power and arm yourself with pro or contra arguments.

Als Vorbereitung auf die Inszenierung der Demonstration lesen die Schülerinnen und Schüler den Text „Nuclear plants blooming" von John Vidal (Worksheet 22, S. 40) und arbeiten die in ihm dargestellten Pro- und Contraargumente heraus. Selbstverständlich können die Schüler auch Argumente, die über den Text hinausgehen, in die Diskussion einbringen. Bei der Inszenierung übernimmt ein Schüler die Rolle eines Reporters, der die einzelnen Demonstranten zu einer Stellungnahme auffordert. Auch sollten Diskussionen zwischen den Demonstranten angeregt werden.
Alternativ zu dem szenischen Spiel könnte die Umwälzung der Argumente auch in Form einer Kugellagerdiskussion (Method Sheet 24, S. 47) erfolgen, wobei mindestens drei Gesprächsrunden anzusetzen sind. Während die Schüler in den ersten zwei Runden jeweils einmal die Position der Befürworter und einmal die Position der Gegner einnehmen, äußern sie in der dritten Runde ihre eigene Meinung.

Task 5: Read George Bush's speech about climate change to find out about his attitude towards global warming. Sit down on the "hot seat" as Bush's spokesperson for environmental issues and ask the spokesperson any questions you have concerning Bush's global warming policy.

Die Schülerinnen und Schüler fassen die Hauptaussagen der Rede Bushs zur Bekämpfung der globalen Erwärmung zusammen und setzen sich kritisch mit seinen Plänen auseinander (Worksheet 23, S. 43). Der Hot seat (Method Sheet 24, S. 47) stellt eine Vertiefung dieser kritischen Auseinandersetzung dar.

Advert "Eastpak"

1. Describe the picture to your partner, who will try to draw it according to your description. Compare his/her drawing to the original.

2. A traditional model to help create any kind of advertising is the **AIDA** principle: gain **A**ttention, hold **I**nterest, arouse **D**esire, and then encourage the reader to take **A**ction. Analyse and evaluate the advertisement with reference to the AIDA formula.
In your opinion, is the advertisement effective? Explain why or why not.

3. Design an advertisement for a product of your choice. In your advertisement refer to global warming somehow or other. Use the principles of the AIDA formula.
As in an exhibition pin your advertisements to the wall. Walk around and have a close look at all the different pieces of work. Discuss which advertisement is the most convincing. Explain why.

2. Eastpack – Stop global warming

gain **Attention**

- the slogan "Stop global warming"
- the three polar bears dressed up as environmental activists and delivering speeches on the threat of global warming

hold **Interest**

- The scene depicted in the advertisement represents a kind of riddle the reader feels curious to solve.

arouse **Desire**

Rational reasons

- Eastpak's products are "BUILT TO RESIST".
- The fact that Eastpak's products are "built to resist" is reflected in and therefore proved by the persistence of the polar bears giving their speeches – *2112 Speeches. No feedback. Still giving Speeches.*

Emotional reasons

- Eastpak refers to global warming, a topic that is touched upon in the headlines. By giving the impression of being concerned about it Eastpak is trying to create a positive, i.e. environmentally-committed image of itself as a company. Buying Eastpak's products implies supporting their concern about and commitment to the environment.

take **Action**

- The product, a bag, is shown.
- Eastpak's internet address is given.
- Global warming being a problem that has to be dealt with urgently, the reader is enticed to buy Eastpak's products.

How to describe pictures

Describe the picture systematically:

1. First of all, give an outline of the picture by describing roughly what is in the foreground, the centre and the background.

2. Now describe the picture in detail. Start with the main subject. Then go on by describing the foreground, the centre and the background in detail.

Useful phrases
The picture/photo presents/shows …
In the centre of the picture/photo …
In the middle …
In the foreground …
In the background …
In the bottom right-hand corner …
In the top right-hand corner …
In the bottom left-hand corner …
In the top left-hand corner …

✂- -

How to create an advertisement – AIDA

The AIDA model provides various principles for creating advertisements.

A = Attention
Make sure your advertisement catches the reader's attention. Possible means are eye-catching slogans or pictures. You can for example ask a question, make an offer, quote a statistic, show intriguing pictures. Use colour and size to increase the attention-grabbing effect.

I = Interest
Once you have got the reader's attention you shouldn't lose it again. By building on the idea or message of your headline try to provoke further interest in your product by e.g. telling a story, cracking a joke, making up a riddle.

D = Desire
Now that the reader is interested you have to create a strong desire to possess your product. Emphasize the various unique advantages your product has for the customer's life. Give rational (e.g. price, technical features) and emotional reasons (e.g. the product as a status symbol) why the customer should buy your product.

A = Action
You must finally encourage the reader to buy your product. Show the product. Tell them where they can purchase it. Indicate your address, your phone number or your web site and tell the reader to contact you. Limit your offer. Offer bonuses. Tell the customer to buy your product now.

How to evaluate a presentation

	What I liked	What I didn't like	What I suggest
Content • informative • clear • concise • interesting • up-to-date • etc.			
Structure • clear • logical • etc.			
Visual aids and materials used • functional • adequate number • varied • etc.			
Language • appropriate • correct • varied • etc.			
Body language • movement • gestures • eye contact • etc.			
Voice • clear articulation • volume • vocal variations • etc.			
Time management			

John Vidal

Eye of the storm

Britain's 'wind rush' – the world's fastest expansion of renewable energy – has created a wave of protest. Are these farms the cure for global warming, or a blight on the landscape?

[...] Britain is right at the start of what is being called the "wind rush", and rural communities are being convulsed by arguments for and against wind technology. Encouraged by the government, which has set targets of generating 10% of all British electricity from renewables by 2010 and is heavily backing developers with grants and subsidies, large companies are piling in with ambitious plans for most of Britain's highlands. [...]

The 1,034 turbines already running produce about 700MW of electricity – about as much as one conventional power station – but over the next seven years more than 7,000MW of generating power will be installed on 73 new farms. It will be the greatest and fastest expansion of renewable energy attempted anywhere in the world – a suitable response, says the government, to global warming. This year 22 new farms with a capacity of 475MW will be built. Next year there will be even more – but instead of the 100ft high machines now dotted around Wales, the west country and Scotland, the industry is moving to 300-, even 400-footers, each generating enough electricity for several thousands homes. Dozens of companies are piling in with proposals.

Plans are in place to move much of the building out to sandbanks and shallow water off the coasts from 2007 onwards. Fifteen giant offshore farms will be built, in the Thames estuary, the Wash, and off the northwest and Welsh coasts. Each could have up to 500 of the biggest turbines in the world, generating potentially 4,5MW each – more if the technology moves on as expected. Altogether 9,000MW of new wind power is planned, enough to meet the government target of 10%. By 2020 the government wants 20% of Britain's energy to come from renewables.

But the proposed farms are provoking fierce opposition from an increasingly organised countryside lobby, which claims that wind power is not green, will not contribute to the fight against global warming and will wreck the countryside. More than 60 national and local groups, led by some of Britain's highest profile conservationists, are now hounding the planners, whipping up antagonism, and undermining the arguments for switching to renewables. As the propaganda war against wind farms heats up, the green movement finds itself split.

"Wind power is sheer lunacy," argues the conservationist David Bellamy, who opposes all British wind developments on the grounds that they can kill birds and destroy countryside. "They can only work for 30% of the time," he says. "How are people going to be able to boil their kettles, or how are we to power our hospitals the rest of the time? It means we have to keep our other stations running in reserve, pouring out carbon dioxide and sulphur dioxide. If they were producing a decent amount of power I would back them. But if you lagged the roofs of 500 homes it would have the effect of putting up one wind turbine. That is what we should be doing."

He also argues that they are a planning fiasco. "If I wanted to build in an area of outstanding natural beauty I wouldn't be allowed. Yet these turbines are 22 storeys high and put on hills where everyone can see them. They need 1,000 tonnes of concrete and a road infrastructure. It beggars belief that some environmental groups say they are 'green'."

The anti-wind lobby took off in 1992 with a group called Country Guardian, which was worried by wind power's potential to damage landscape. [...]

to be convulsed to be torn between

subsidy financial support
to pile in to come in large numbers

to be dotted around to be spread over an area

shallow not deep

to wreck to destroy

to hound to harass
antagonism hostility
to undermine to weaken

sheer complete

a decent amount enough
to lag to insulate

to beggar belief to be too extreme to believe

The core of the antis' argument is that wind power is expensive and will achieve little. "Why are we building wind turbines and paying three times the odds for their electricity when other options are so obvious? Why are we building the biggest passenger jet the world has ever seen? Why do we not reward people for saving energy?" says Dr John Etherington, a retired academic regarded as the intellectual guru of Country Guardian.

This leaves Greenpeace, Friends of the Earth and WWF, with more than 70,000 members between them, in the unusual position of defending multinational companies and the government, and trying to debunk what they call the myths put out by the antis. Tony Juniper, director of Friends of the Earth, says that the opposition exaggerates shamelessly and dangerously.

"They are parochial, short-sighted, selfish, peddling falsehoods and misconceptions," he says. "Climate change is no longer a theory. It is the world's most pressing environmental problem, and the anti-lobby, helped by nuclear interests, is trying to undermine Britain's role as a leader in tackling it and to fatally delay action. Wind is the most advanced of all the renewable technologies, but it needs to be followed quickly by solar, wave, biomass and others," he says. "No one is arguing that wind generators should cover all the national parks. That would be mad. The landscape can and must be protected."

The opposition is using every argument imaginable. Its websites claim that house prices fall near farms, that turbine noise, infrasound and the flicker of blades can drive people and animals mad, that bats die in great numbers, job figures are inflated, tourists are put off, and even that horses bolt near them.

One of the strongest arguments used is that every farm is liable to kill thousands of birds, including hundreds of golden eagles, kites and other rare species. The RSPB, which supports wind power, says it objects only when there is "insufficient information about the risks to birds and their habitats to conclude that there will not be a problem." The British Wind Energy association, the industry lobby group, is perplexed. "Even in Altamont Pass in America, where 7,000 turbines were erected on a migratory route, it was only 0.2 birds per turbine per year. Compare this with the number killed by cats, cars and by flying into windows, or even by global warming, and it is not significant at all," a spokesman says.

The antis "are a well-organised small minority," says Allan Moore, chair of the British wind energy association and head of renewables at National Wind Power. In the next 10 years he expects to invest almost $1.7bn in wind. Moore spent 30 years building and installing nuclear coal, gas and other power stations before moving to wind. "Proportion is needed. In the 17th century we had 90,000 windmills in Britain. They were a part of life. What we're looking to do is install perhaps 4,000, making 5,000 in total. Roughly half will be onshore and half offshore. If 4,000 turbines sounds a lot, compare Germany, where last year alone they installed more than 2,500MW of capacity and now have 7,000 turbines."

Wind, he says, is not the only answer to producing clean electricity or combating global warming. "What wind is about is displacing fossil fuels, saving carbon and greenhouse gases. That is the driver. Every kilowatt of wind power generated is one less of polluting power. The wind industry can do a lot quickly. If in 30 years' time someone comes up with something better, we'll take the turbines away."

The future, he accepts, will be a mixture of tidal power, solar, biomass and other renewables, "but these technologies have some way to go and are where wind energy was 12–15 years ago. I think ultimately we'll be using many sorts of power."

Guardian Weekly, May 28 – June 3, 2004, pp. 15–16

three times the odds three times as much

to debunk to show that sth is false

parochial only concerned with small issues that happen in your local area and not interested in more important things
to peddle to spread

flicker small sudden movements
blade *Turbinenschaufel*
to bolt to run away because you are frightened
to be liable to do sth to be likely to do sth
kite a bird of the hawk family
RSPB Royal Society for the Protection of Birds

1. Global warming is regarded as one of the main problems the world faces today and will face in future. Therefore solutions are urgently needed. What solutions are currently suggested to fight global warming? Have a look at the cartoon dealing with global warming and possible solutions. What solutions are referred to in the cartoon? Think of arguments put forward by the supporters of wind power and of nuclear power.

2. Try to find out about wind technology in Germany. How many wind turbines have already been installed? What percentage of all German electricity do they generate? …
Use the Internet. Helpful websites to get the most up-to-date information:

- de.wikipedia.org/wiki/Windenergie
- www.erneuerbare-energien.de/inhalt (Bundesministerium für Umwelt, Naturschutz und Reaktorsicherheit)
- www.wind-energie.de (Bundesverband WindEnergie e.V.)
- www.deutsche-windindustrie.de (Die Windindustrie in Deutschland)
- www.dewi.de (Deutsches Windenergie-Institut)

3. Describe the British situation and compare it to the situation in Germany.

4. Make a list of the pro and contra arguments.

5. In Wales, two young farmers, Geraint Davies and Robin Williams, applied for permission to establish a wind farm on their land close to Snowdonia National Park. They found sympathizers for their plan and opponents.

Sympathizers	Opponents
• Geraint Davies and Robin Williams	• Country Guardian
• Friends of the Earth	• North Wales Tourism
• The British Wind energy association	• The National Trust
• members of the local council	• members of the local council

Imagine that these groups take part in a local council meeting where the request of the two farmers is discussed and decided. The class is divided into sympathizers and opponents. Individual students will prepare statements on behalf of the people and groups mentioned above. Each person or group will be allowed to give a statement, which should be discussed controversially. At the end of the council meeting a vote will be taken whether the request should be granted or not.

6. Write a newspaper report about the local council meeting.

7. Find out more about other renewable energies: hydro power, solar power, biomass energy, geothermal energy. Present the information to your classmates.
Use the Internet to collect information. Useful websites are:

- www.greenpeace.org
- www.wwf.org
- www.foe.org

1. Possible solutions currently discussed to combat global warming
- Renewable energies, e.g. hydro power, wind power, solar power, biomass energy and geothermal energy
- Nuclear power
- Carbon sequestration (= storage of carbon underground)
- Cap and trade (= trading of carbon emissions)

2. Wind technology in Germany (2006)
- By 2020 the German government wants 20 % of Germany's energy to be produced by renewables and 50 % by the middle of this century.
- At the end of June 2006 18054 turbines were installed, producing 19299MW of electricity, i.e. 6.8 % of Germany's electric power consumption.

3. Wind power – the situation in Great Britain (2004)
- The government has set targets for generating 10 % of all British electricity from renewables by 2010.
- By 2020 the government wants 20 % of Britain's energy to be produced by renewables.
- 1,034 turbines already running produce about 700MW of electricity.
- Over the next seven years 73 new farms will be installed generating 7,000MW of energy.
- On a long-term basis 9,000MW of electricity generated by wind power is planned, enough to meet the government's target of 10 %.
- Instead of the 100ft high machines, the industry will gradually install 300- and 400-footers, each generating enough electricity for several thousand homes.
- From 2007 onwards more and more wind farms will be built on sandbanks and in shallow water off the coasts: 15 off-shore farms are already planned to be built in the Thames estuary, the Wash, and off the northwest and Welsh coasts.
- Compared to Germany, which according to Vidal had 7,000 turbines in 2004, Great Britain with 1,034 lagged far behind as far as wind power is concerned.

4. Pros

Wind power …
- is one answer to tackle today's most pressing environmental problem: global warming;
- replaces power generated by fossil fuels, thereby reduces the emissions of carbon and other greenhouse gases;
- is the most advanced of all renewable technologies;
- can be installed quickly;
- will be replaced by solar, wave, tidal, biomass and other renewables in future;
- does not destroy the landscape significantly;
- does not kill birds and destroy their habitats in a disproportionate way;
- in Great Britain is not as developed as in Germany, where 7,000 turbines have already been installed so far, compared to a planned 5,000 in total in Great Britain.

Cons

Wind power …
- can only work for 30 % of the time so that other stations would have to be kept running in reserve, pouring out carbon dioxide and sulphur dioxide;
- doesn't produce a sufficient amount of power;
- is expensive;
- wrecks the countryside as turbines are 22 storeys high, situated on hills where everyone can see them, need tonnes of concrete and a road infrastructure;
- makes house prices fall near wind farms;
- puts tourists off;
- affects people and animals insofar as the turbine noise, infrasound and the flicker of blades irritates people and animals;
- kills birds (e.g. golden eagles, kites and other rare species) as well as bats in great numbers.

Useful phrases for discussions

Starting a discussion
I'd like to know …
Could you tell me …
What do you think of …
What I'm interested in is …

Making suggestions
Let's …
What about …
Why don't we/you …
I suggest that we/you …
Wouldn't it be better to …

Listing and contrasting arguments
First of all, …
The main reason is …
The most important point is …
Secondly, …/Thirdly …
Another reason is …/Besides that, …/
Furthermore, …/Moreover, …
And finally, …/Last, but not least, …/
To conclude …/To summarize …
On the one hand …, on the other hand …
In contrast to/with …

Explaining
Let me explain/tell you …
Let me illustrate my point.
Let me put it another way, …
…, in other words …
There are a number of reasons why …

Interrupting
Sorry, but …
Excuse me for interrupting you, but …
Can I just say something here?
I would like to add something here.
May I ask a question?

Giving your opinion
In my opinion …
Personally speaking, I think/I believe that …
If you ask me …
The way I see it is …/I take the view that …
As far as I'm concerned …

Expressing agreement
I completely agree with you.
You're absolutely right.
That's a convincing argument.
That seems to be a great idea.
There's no doubt about this.

Expressing disagreement
I disagree/don't agree with you.
That's totally wrong.
I'm not convinced at all.
I don't see your point.
I don't think you realise that …

Asking for clarification
Could you repeat your last point, please?
What do you exactly mean by that?
I didn't quite follow what you said about …
Prove it!
What about the facts?

How to analyse and write a newspaper report

Analysing a newspaper report

A **news story** should always be an objective report, i.e. it should be based on facts and not be influenced by the reporter's opinion or feelings. However, pure objectivity is not always possible. By selecting facts to be included in the report, by using one word instead of another, by writing in a certain tone the reporter reveals his attitude towards the reported issue. But at least a reporter should try to present the facts in the most factual way possible.
The kind of report in which the journalist explicitly wants to express his opinion is called an **editorial** or **leader**. In contrast to the news story, the aim of which is mainly to inform the reader, the purpose of the editorial is to influence the reader, i.e. to convince the reader of a certain opinion.

Newspaper reports generally consist of 3 parts:

1. The **headline** is intended to
- catch the reader's eye.
- arouse the reader's interest.
- inform the reader about an interesting aspect of the story.

2. The **lead** – one or more opening paragraphs –
- summarizes the news of the following story.
- generally answers the four w's (*Who*? *What*? *Where*? *When*?).

3. The **body**
- provides the reader with detailed information. Apart from the four w's, which are answered in greater detail, the body often informs the reader about *how* and *why* the story happened.
  In an editorial the body contains a highly subjective analysis of the subject.

The way the information is generally structured in a news report is often referred to as an **inverted pyramid**, the most important and interesting information coming first, followed by information of gradually decreasing importance and interest.

Writing a newspaper report

When writing a newspaper report bear in mind the following rules:
- Divide your report into 3 parts: the headline, the lead, the body.
- Divide the body into short paragraphs, each dealing with one aspect of the story.
- Give information in a clear, concise, accurate, and complete way.
- Answer the 6 questions *Who? What? Where? When? Why? How?*.
- Start with the most important and most interesting information and continue with information of less importance and interest.
- Use the past tense to describe events that have already happened.
- Use direct speech or reported speech when referring to what people said.

John Vidal

Nuclear plants blooming

Global warming is giving the n-word a second chance.

Nuclear power is back on the march. It has been reviled and rejected for 25 years as man's most dangerous and unsustainable fuel source, but its friends are now billing it as the only practical way of countering climate change, oil shocks and landscape destruction in the west.

So, is it possible that public opinion is wrong, and that nuclear should be the fuel of choice of the future?

Absolutely, says Tony Blair, who last month told MPs that America was pressing Britain to re-examine the case for building a new generation of nuclear power stations. Nuclear must stay on the agenda "if you are serious about the issue of climate change".

Definitely, says the independent scientist James Lovelock, who has repeated his lifelong support for nuclear energy and recently argued that civilisation is in "imminent danger" from global warming and must use nuclear power – "the one safe, available, energy source" – to avoid catastrophe.

Perhaps, say some of Britain's leading environmental thinkers, who are calling for a debate about whether nuclear needs to be reassessed, and whether it should even be compared to other forms of renewable energy.

Electricity generation is responsible for about one third of worldwide greenhouse gases and, according to the UN's International Atomic Energy Agency (IAEA), nuclear power, which provides 16% of the worlds electricity, saves roughly 600 m tonnes of carbon emissions per year. This is almost twice the total amount the so far unratified global warming Kyoto Protocol treaty is designed to save.

On emissions, nuclear compares well with renewables, says the agency. The nuclear power chain, from uranium mining to waste disposal and including reactor and construction emits roughly 2–6 grams of carbon per kilowatt-hour. This, it says, is about the same as wind and solar power, and two orders of magnitude below coal, oil and even natural gas.

With world electricity demand expected to increase at least 30% and possibly up to 100% on 1990 figures by 2020, the World Nuclear Association says nuclear is now not just an option but a necessity for survival. "With carbon emissions threatening the very stability of the biosphere, the security of our world requires a massive transformation to clean energy," says Ian Hore-Lacy of the London-based lobby group. [...]

Nuclear now has powerful advocates around government who say it is the best way to survive climate change. "One advantage is that the technology is known," says Sir John Houghton, former head of the Met Office and the UN's intercontinental panel on climate change, in a new edition of Global Warming, the Complete Briefing. "They can be built now and therefore contribute to the reduction of carbon dioxide emissions ... estimates are that the cost of nuclear electricity is similar to the cost of electricity from natural gas when the additional cost of capture and sequestration of carbon dioxide is added." [...]

Other environmentalists, traditionally hostile to nuclear, say that growing understanding of climate change is leading them to question old assumptions. "It's important that environmentalists don't become fundamentalists [just] following the 1970s line," says Paul Allen, development director at the Centre for Alternative Technology in Machynlleth. "We've got to look at all the arguments. We have to engage in the debate. Nuclear is one of the arguments that must be considered. We should not just write it off."

to revile to criticize
unsustainable sth that cannot be continued at the same level
to bill to advertise
imminent likely to happen soon
to reassess to reconsider
unratified not officially valid
panel a group of specialists
sequestration the capturing of carbon dioxide and its storage underground
assumption belief

Denisa Kukucova picks sunflowers near Slovaika's oldest nuclear power plant, Jaslovske Bohunice

Allen says he is not endorsing nuclear, but is trying to keep an open mind. Nuclear costs, he says, must include the security, insurance, decommissioning, long-term storage and waste disposal costs, as well as the energy needed to build the plants. "For me [nuclear] is not a winner, but let's do the calculations," he says.

The IAEA does not believe that nuclear power can grow fast enough to combat global warming. Last month, as part of the celebrations for 50 years of civil nuclear power, director general Dr Mohamed El Baradei said that even if the global economy grew strongly, nuclear power would only grow about 70 % over the next 25 years and its share of world energy would proportionately fall because of the more rapid expansion of other electricity sources.

He concluded that for the rural poor in developing countries, off-grid, small-scale, localised renewables are the best power solution, but that nuclear suited the needs of big, expanding cities, and countries with large centralised power generation.

But a global nuclear programme, of the scale needed to push its share well ahead of other forms of fossil fuel electricity generation, could cost hundreds of billions of dollars to get up and running and has little likelihood of attracting private finance. Safety fears have been a problem since Three Mile Island 1979 and Chernobyl in 1986.

Nuclear stations usually take eight to 15 years to build, and almost that long to start repaying their financial and carbon investments. "The simple solution is that renewables and energy conservation can deliver the cuts immediately," says a Greenpeace spokesman. "All it needs is political will."

Even if nuclear were the best option to tackle global warming, it's likely to fail again on cost grounds, says the Rocky Mountain Institute, the US energy consultant that advises governments and big companies.

"Capital is finite," says a spokesman. "Each dollar invested in electric efficiency displaces nearly seven times as much carbon dioxide as a dollar invested in nuclear power, without any nasty side effects. If climate change is the problem, nuclear power isn't the solution."

Guardian Weekly, August 20 – 26, 2004, p. 19

to endorse to promote

to decommission to officially stop using a nuclear power station

off-grid *unabhängig vom Netz*

scale size

to deliver to provide, to supply

Make a list of the arguments in favour of and against the building of nuclear power plants.

Pros

Nuclear power ...

- is the only practical way of countering climate change, oil shocks and landscape destruction by windmill farms;
- is a safe and available energy source;
- saves 600m tonnes of carbon emissions each year (twice the amount the Kyoto treaty is intended to save);
- compares with renewable energy such as wind and solar power as far as carbon emissions are concerned;
- emits far less carbon per kilowatt-hour than power generated by coal, oil or natural gas;
- is based on well-known technology;
- generates electricity at a similar cost to natural gas.

Cons

Nuclear power ...

- includes massive costs for security, insurance, decommissioning, long-term storage, waste-disposal costs and the energy needed to build the plants;
- cannot grow fast enough to combat global warming;
- doesn't suit everybody's needs, i.e. it suits the needs of big, expanding cities, and countries with large centralised power generation, but not the needs of the rural poor in developing countries;
- has little likelihood of attracting private finance in view of the fact that the establishment of a global nuclear programme would imply enormous costs;
- is unsafe, e.g. Chernobyl (1986);
- takes a long time to be installed as nuclear power stations take very long to be built (8–15 years) and therefore only repay their financial and carbon investments much later.

George Bush announces clear skies and global climate change initiatives

National Oceanic and Atmospheric Administration, Silver Spring, Maryland

Thank you very much for that warm welcome. It's an honour to join you all today to talk about our environment and about the prospect of dramatic progress to improve it.

Today, I'm announcing a new environmental approach that will clean our skies, bring greater health to our citizens and encourage environmentally responsible development in America and around the world. [...]

America and the world share this common goal: we must foster economic growth in ways that protect our environment. We must encourage growth that will provide a better life for citizens, while protecting the land, the water, and the air that sustain life.

In pursuit of this goal, my government has set two priorities: we must clean our air, and we must address the issue of global climate change. We must also act in a serious and responsible way, given the scientific uncertainties. While these uncertainties remain, we can begin now to address the human factors that contribute to climate change. Wise action now is an insurance policy against future risks.

I have been working with my Cabinet to meet these challenges with forward and creative thinking. I said, if need be, let's challenge the status quo. But let's always remember, let's do what is in the interest of the American people.

Today, I'm confident that the environmental path that I announce will benefit the entire world. This new approach is based on this common-sense idea: that economic growth is key to environmental progress, because it is growth that provides the resources for investment in clean technologies.

This new approach will harness the power of markets, the creativity of entrepreneurs, and draw upon the best scientific research. And it will make possible a new partnership with the developing world to meet our common environmental and economic goals.

We will apply this approach first to the challenge of cleaning the air that Americans breathe. [...]

Now, global climate change presents a different set of challenges and requires a different strategy. The science is more complex, the answers are less certain, and the technology is less developed. So we need a flexible approach that can adjust to new information and new technology.

I reaffirm America's commitment to the United Nations Framework Convention and its central goal, to stabilise atmospheric greenhouse gas concentrations at a level that will prevent dangerous human interference with the climate. Our immediate goal is to reduce America's greenhouse gas emissions relative to the size of our economy.

My administration is committed to cutting our nation's greenhouse gas intensity – how much we emit per unit of economic activity – by 18% over the next 10 years. This will set America on a path to slow the growth of our greenhouse gas emissions and, as science justifies, to stop and then reverse the growth of emissions.

This is the common sense way to measure progress. Our nation must have economic growth – growth to create opportunity; growth to create a higher quality of life for our citizens. Growth is also what pays for investments in clean technologies, increased conservation, and energy efficiency. Meeting our commitment

to foster to encourage/ to promote

to sustain to provide enough of what sb/sth needs in order to live

status quo the situation as it is now or as it was before a recent change

to harness to control

to reduce our greenhouse gas intensity by 18 % by the year 2012 will prevent over 500 m metric tons of greenhouse gases from going into the atmosphere over the course of the decade. And that is the equivalent of taking 70 m cars off the road.
To achieve this goal, our nation must move forward on many fronts, looking at every sector of our economy. We will challenge American businesses to further reduce emissions. Already, agreements with the semiconductor and aluminium industries and others have dramatically cut emissions of some of the most potent greenhouse gases. We will build on these successes with new agreements and greater reductions.
Our government will also move forward immediately to create world-class standards for measuring and registering emission reductions. And we will give transferable credits to companies that can show real emission reductions.
We will promote renewable energy production and clean coal technology, as well as nuclear power, which produces no greenhouse gas emissions. And we will work to safely improve fuel economy for our cars and our trucks.
Overall, my budget devotes $ 4.5 billion to addressing climate change – more than any other nation's commitment in the entire world. This is an increase of more than $ 700 m over last year's budget. Our nation will continue to lead the world in basic climate and science research to address gaps in our knowledge that are important to decision makers.
When we make decisions, we want to make sure we do so on sound science; not what sounds good, but what is real. And the United States leads the world in providing that kind of research. We'll devote $ 588 m towards the research and development of energy conservation technologies. We must and we will conserve more in the United States. And we will spend $ 408 m toward research and development on renewables, on renewable energy.
This funding includes $ 150 m for an initiative that Spence Abraham laid out the other day, $ 150 m for the Freedom Car Initiative, which will advance the prospect of breakthrough zero-emission fuel cell technologies.
My comprehensive energy plan, the first energy plan that any administration has put out in a long period of time, provides $ 4.6 bn over the next five years in clean energy tax incentives to encourage purchases of hybrid and fuel cell vehicles, to promote residential solar energy, and to reward investments in wind, solar and biomass energy production. And we will look for ways to increase the amount of carbon stored by America's farms and forests through a strong conservation title in the farm bill. I have asked Secretary Veneman to recommend new targeted incentives for landowners to increase carbon storage.
By doing all these things, by giving companies incentives to cut emissions, by diversifying our energy supply to include cleaner fuels, by increasing conservation, by increasing research and development and tax incentives for energy efficiency and clean technologies, and by increasing carbon storage, I am absolutely confident that America will reach the goal that I have set.
If, however, by 2012, our progress is not sufficient and sound science justifies further action, the United States will respond with additional measures that may include broad-based market programmes as well as additional incentives and voluntary measures designed to accelerate technology development and deployment.
Addressing global climate change will require a sustained effort over many generations. My approach recognizes that economic growth is the solution, not the

semiconductor *Halbleiter*

credit money

to devote to give an amount of money to sb/sth

sound reliable

incentive sth that encourages you to do sth
residential at home

title *Gesetzesbezeichnung*

deployment effective use

problem. Because a nation that grows its economy is a nation that can afford investments and new technologies.

The approach taken under the Kyoto protocol would have required the United States to make deep and immediate cuts in our economy to meet an arbitrary target. It would have cost our economy up to $ 400 bn and we would have lost 4.9 m jobs.

arbitrary not seeming to be based on reason, a system or plan

As President of the United States, charged with safeguarding the welfare of the American people and American workers, I will not commit our nation to an unsound international treaty that will throw millions of our citizens out of work. [...]

To clean the air, and to address climate change, we need to recognize that economic growth and environmental protection go hand in hand. Affluent societies are the ones that demand, and can therefore afford, the most environmental protection. Prosperity is what allows us to commit more and more resources to environmental protection. And in the coming decades, the world needs to develop and deploy billions of dollars of technologies that generate energy in cleaner ways. And we need strong economic growth to make that possible.

affluent rich, wealthy

Americans are among the most creative people in our history. We have used radio waves to peer into the deepest reaches of space. We cracked life's genetic code. We have made our air and land and water significantly cleaner, even as we have built the world's strongest economy.

to peer to look closely

When I see what Americans have done, I know what we can do. We can tap the power of economic growth to further protect our environment for generations that follow. And that's what we're going to do.

to tap *erschließen*

Thank you.

www.whitehouse.gov/news/releases/2002/02/20020214-5.html

Summarize George Bush's plans to tackle global warming and explain why environmental campaigners such as Greenpeace accuse Bush of committing climate crimes.

George Bush's strategy to tackle global warming

- to immediately reduce America's greenhouse gas emissions relative to the size of its economy, i.e. to reduce America's greenhouse gas intensity (= how much America emits per unit of economic growth) by 18 % by the year 2012
- to foster economic growth as it pays for investments in clean technologies
- to challenge American businesses to further reduce emissions
- to create world-class standards in order to measure and register emissions reductions
- to give transferable emissions credits to companies that can show real emission reductions
- to promote renewable energy production, clean coal technology and nuclear power
- to improve fuel economy for cars and trucks
- to spend $ 4.5 billion on combating climate change
- to lead the world in basic climate and science research, devoting $ 588 m towards the research and development of energy conservation technologies and $ 408 towards research on and development of renewable energy
- to promote zero-emission fuel cell technologies
- to provide clean energy tax incentives in order to encourage the purchase of hybrid and fuel cell vehicles, to promote residential solar energy, and to reward investments in wind, solar and biomass energy production
- to provide incentives for America's farms and forests to increase carbon storage

Why do environmental campaigners accuse him of committing climate crimes?

Generally, environmental activists accuse Bush of not addressing the problem of global warming appropriately neither on a national nor on an international level although the US is the world's largest producer of greenhouse gas emissions.

As far as his global warming speech is concerned he is criticised for the following:

- Bush's proposed 18 % reduction in emissions intensity by the year 2012 will actually allow net emissions to rise at nearly the same rate as at present rather than fall.
- Bush doesn't suggest anything beyond voluntary action by companies to reduce their greenhouse gas emissions.
- Bush's proposed budget devoted to address climate change is not significantly higher than recent budgets.
- Bush rejects the Kyoto protocol calling it an unsound international treaty, which has unrealistic goals and could damage the US economy. At the same time he doesn't offer any ideas of how to improve the Kyoto protocol.
- Bush stresses the quoted scientific uncertainties unduly to justify not taking further action to curb greenhouse gas emissions.

Pyramid discussion

Eine Pyramidendiskussion verläuft in mehreren Phasen. Am Anfang steht eine Einzelarbeit. Die Ergebnisse der Einzelarbeit werden in Partnerarbeit diskutiert, wobei sich die jeweiligen Partner auf ein Arbeitsergebnis einigen. Dieses wird anschließend einem weiteren Paar vorgestellt, und diese Vierergruppe formuliert nun wiederum eine gemeinsame Position usw. Die Pyramidendiskussion ist dann beendet, wenn die gesamte Gruppe ein Endergebnis gemeinsam festgelegt hat.

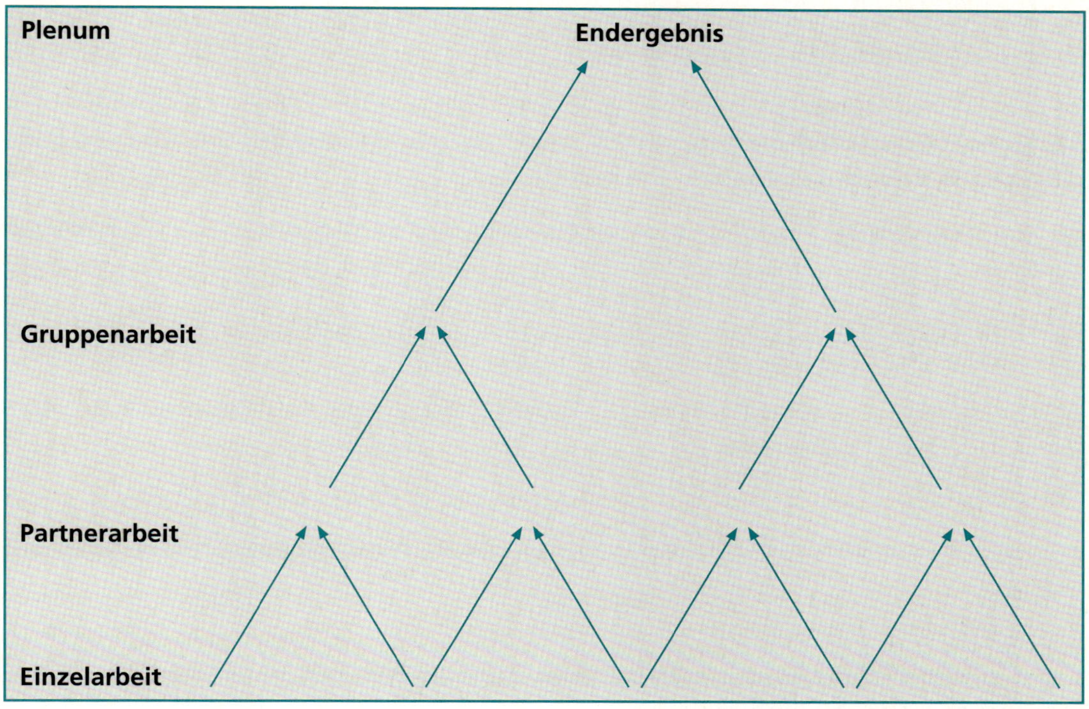

Kugellagerdiskussion (double circle discussion)

Die Schüler setzen oder stellen sich in zwei Kreisen – einem Innenkreis und einem Außenkreis – paarweise gegenüber und diskutieren ein vorgegebenes Thema. Nach einigen Minuten bewegt sich der Innen- oder der Außenkreis um eine oder zwei Positionen weiter, sodass die Schüler neuen Partnern gegenüberstehen und mit diesen diskutieren können. Dieser Vorgang kann beliebig wiederholt werden.

Hot seat

Einzelne Schüler schlüpfen in die Rolle einer bestimmten Person (fiktiv oder non-fiktiv) und nehmen auf einem Stuhl – dem Hot seat – Platz, um sich dort den teilweise auch kritischen Fragen ihrer Mitschüler zu stellen. Es empfiehlt sich, die Fragen vorbereiten zu lassen.

Aspect 4: Over to you – What you can do

Task 1: Read the excerpt from the book *The weather makers* written by Tim Flannery (2005) and make a list of the tips he offers to combat global warming.

Die von Tim Flannery vorgeschlagenen Maßnahmen zur Reduzierung der globalen Erwärmung werden aus dem Text (Worksheet 25, S. 49) herausgearbeitet und durch weitere von den Schülerinnen und Schülern genannte Handlungsmöglichkeiten ergänzt. Anschließend werden alle Maßnahmen ihrer Wichtigkeit entsprechend hierarchisch geordnet. Dies könnte das Ergebnis einer Pyramidendiskussion sein (vgl. Method Sheet 24, S. 47). Zum Abschluss sollten konkrete eigene Handlungsmöglichkeiten diskutiert werden.

Task 2: Carry out a survey to find out how "energy efficient" people are. Present the data you have collected in graphs, charts and tables. Discuss the results.

Die Schülerinnen und Schüler ergänzen die von *Friends of the Earth* erstellte Umfrage (Worksheet 26, S. 52) durch zwei eigene Fragen und führen sie in Partner- oder Gruppenarbeit in der Schule oder zu Hause durch, wobei eine verbindliche Mindestanzahl von Befragungen festgelegt werden sollte. Sie werten die Ergebnisse aus, präsentieren sie in Form von Grafiken, Schaubildern und Tabellen vor der Klasse und kommentieren bzw. diskutieren sie (vgl. Strategy Sheet 10, S. 22).
Die angekreuzten Antworten stellen die „umweltfreundlichen" Antworten dar. Je mehr die Antworten der Befragten mit diesen übereinstimmen, desto energiebewusster sind sie. Um den Schülern die Auswertung der Umfrage zu erleichtern, sollten die Fragen und Antworten mit den Schülern vor der Durchführung der Umfrage durchgesprochen werden.
Hinweis: Die hellgrau gedruckten Antworten (x) sollten getilgt werden oder der Kopierer sollte vor der Vervielfältigung auf hell eingestellt werden.

Task 3: Launch an information campaign about global warming in general but in particular about how everybody can contribute to tackle this problem.

Die Schülerinnen und Schüler planen eine Informationskampagne zum Thema „Global warming" und führen sie durch (Strategy Sheet 27, S. 53). Dabei greifen sie auf Informationen der gesamten Einheit zurück. Der Schwerpunkt der Informationskampagne sollte jedoch auf den Lösungsmöglichkeiten liegen (vgl. Aspect 3 und Aspect 4).

Task 4: Imagine you take part in an art project about today's climate and energy policy. Create a "piece of art" for this project and organize an exhibition.

In Anlehnung an ein von der Kunsthochschule Berlin-Weißensee und der Akademie für Design und Kunst Charkiw (Ukraine) durchgeführtes Projekt mit dem Thema „Visual energy. Nach Tschernobyl – Ressourcen, Energien und wir", das sich mit Tschernobyl und mit Energie- und Klimapolitik beschäftigt, setzen sich die Schülerinnen und Schüler künstlerisch mit diesem Thema auseinander. Bevor sie Arbeiten zu der o.g. Thematik in Angriff nehmen, sollten sie über das Projekt informiert werden. In diesem Zusammenhang wird eine Arbeit eines Studenten der Kunsthochschule Berlin-Weißensee gemeinsam betrachtet und kommentiert (Worksheet 28, S. 53). Die anschließend von den Schülern erstellten Produkte in Form von Plakaten, Büchern, Kinospots, Comics, Web-Seiten, Videoclips, Installationen, Postkartenserien usw. sollten ausgestellt werden. Ein Titel für die Ausstellung sollte gemeinsam gefunden werden. Im Rahmen einer Vernissage, zu der auch die Öffentlichkeit (Mitschüler, Eltern, Freunde usw.) eingeladen werden kann, präsentieren und erläutern die Schüler ihre „Kunstwerke".
Nähere Informationen zu dem Projekt können bei dem Bundesministerium für Umwelt, Naturschutz und Reaktorsicherheit (BMU) – Referat Öffentlichkeitsarbeit, D-11055 Berlin, service@bmu.bund.de, www.bmu.de eingeholt werden.
Hinweis: Bei diesem Projekt bietet es sich an, fächerübergreifend mit dem Fach Kunst zusammenzuarbeiten.

Tim Flannery

Over to you

[...] You can, in a few months rather than the fifty years allowed by some governments, easily attain the 70 percent reduction in emissions required to stabilize the earth's climate. All it takes are a few changes to your personal life, none of which requires serious sacrifices.

Understanding how you use electricity is the most powerful tool in your armory, for that allows you to make effective decisions about reducing your personal emissions of CO_2. To begin, pick up and read carefully your electricity bill. Is your bill higher than it was at the same time last year? If so, why? A phone call or e-mail inquiry to your power supplier may help clarify this.

While you are there, ask about a green power option (where the provider guarantees to source a percentage of power from renewables). The green power option can cost as little as a dollar per week yet is highly effective in reducing emissions. If your provider does not offer a suitable green option, dump them and call a competitor. Changing your power supplier is usually a matter of a single phone call, involving no interruption of supply or inconvenience in billing. If, however, a power monopoly reigns in your area, you need to lobby the authorities to create a free market. It is possible, in switching to green power, to reduce your household emissions to zero. All as the result of a single phone call.

If you wish to take more decisive action, the best place for most people to start is with hot water. In the developed world, roughly one-third of CO_2 emissions result from domestic power, and one-third of a typical domestic power bill is spent on heating water. This is crazy, since the sun will heat your water for free if you have the right device. An initial outlay loan to do so, for in sunny climates like California or southern Europe the payback period is around two or three years, and as the devices usually carry a ten-year guarantee, that means at least seven to eight years of free hot water. Even in cloudy regions such as Germany and Britain, you will get several years' worth of hot water for free.

If you wish to reduce your impact even further, start with the greatest consumers of power, which for most people are air conditioning, heating, and refrigeration. If you are thinking of installing any such items, you should seek out the most energy-efficient model available. A good rule of thumb is to choose the smallest device to suit your average needs, and consider alternatives: It may be cheaper to install insulation rather than buying and running a larger heater or cooler. It can be difficult to convince children that they need to turn off appliances when they are finished with them. One way to teach them is for a family to examine its power bill together and set a target for reduction. When it's met, give the kids the savings.

I became so outraged at the irresponsibility of the coal burners that I decided to generate my own electricity, which has proved to be one of the most satisfying things I've ever done. For the average householder, solar panels are the best way to do so. Twelve 80-watt panels is the number I granted myself, and the amount of power this generates in Australia is sufficient to run the house. To survive on this quantum, however, our family is vigilant about energy use, and we cook with gas. And I'm fitter than before because I use hand tools rather than the electrical variety to make and fix things. Solar panels have a twenty-five-year guarantee (and often last for up to forty years). With the cost of electricity rising, and because I'll be enjoying the free power they provide well into retirement, I view them as a form of superannuation.

armory a place where weapons are kept

to dump to leave

billing preparing and sending bills to customers

device piece of equipment

outlay the money that you have to spend to start a new project

appliances *Haushaltsgeräte*

solar panels a piece of equipment on a roof that uses light and heat energy from the sun to produce hot water and electricity

vigilant watchful

superannuation pension

The town of Schoenau in Germany offers a different example of direct action. Some of its residents were so alarmed by the Chernobyl disaster that they decided to do something to reduce their country's dependence on nuclear power. It started with a group of ten parents who gave prizes for energy savings. This proved so successful that it soon bloomed into a citizens' group determined to wrest control of the town's power supply from KWR, the monopoly that supplied them.

They put together their own study, then raised DM 2 million to build their own green power scheme. Eventually, they raised over DM 6.5 million – enough to purchase the power supply, grid and all, from KWR – and today the town runs not only its own power supply but a successful consulting business that advises on how to "green" the grid right across the country. Each year Schoenau's power supply becomes greener, and even the big power users, such as a plastics recycling factory situated in the town, are happy with the result.

It is not feasible right now for most of us to do away with burning fossil fuels for transport, but we can greatly reduce their use. Walking wherever possible is highly effective, as is taking public transport. Hybrid fuel vehicles are twice as fuel efficient as a standard, similar-sized car, and trading in your four-wheel-drive or SUV for a medium-sized hybrid fuel car cuts your personal transport emissions by 70 percent in one fell swoop. [...]

If enough of us buy green power, solar panels, solar hot water systems, and hybrid vehicles, the cost of these items will plummet. This will encourage the sale of yet more panels and wind generators, and soon the bulk of domestic power will be generated by renewable technologies. This will place sufficient pressure on industry that, when combined with the pressure from Kyoto, will compel energy-hungry enterprises to maximize efficiency and turn to clean power generation. This will make renewables even more affordable. As a result, the developing world – including China and India – will be able to afford clean power rather than filthy coal. [...]

Much could go wrong with this linked lifeline to climate safety. It may be that the big power users will infiltrate governments further and stymie the renewables sector; or maybe we will act too slowly, and nations such as China and India will have already invested in fossil fuel generation before the price of renewables comes down. Or perhaps the rate of climate change will be discovered to be too great and we will have to draw CO_2 from the atmosphere.

As these challenges suggest, we are the generation fated to live in the most interesting of times, for we are now the weather makers, and the future of biodiversity and civilization hangs on our actions. [...]

Tim Flannery: The Weather Makers, Melbourne, Text Publishing Company, 2005, pp. 302–306

to wrest control of sb to take power from sb

grid *Netz*

to do away with sth to stop having sth

swoop a sudden and quick move downwards

to plummet to fall suddenly and quickly

to compel to force

to stymie to obstruct

1. Make a list of the tips Tim Flannery offers for every individual to combat global warming. Can you think of other measures? Add them to the list.

2. Which of the measures to fight global warming do you consider to be most important/least important? Draw up a list ranking the measures.

3. What could you personally do to contribute to the fight against global warming?

1. Measures to combat global warming put forward by Tim Flannery

- Change to green power. In case your power supplier cannot offer you a green power option look for another power supplier.
- Install a solar hot water system.
- Use energy-efficient appliances for air conditioning, heating and refrigeration.
- Install insulation.
- Encourage your family to save energy. Give incentives.
- Fit solar panels on the roof of your home.
- Cook with gas.
- Use hand tools rather than electrical devices to make and repair things.
- Gather information about your village's or town's power supply and about green alternatives. Get politically involved.
- Walk whenever you can or use public transport.
- When buying a new car, check its fuel efficiency.

Other measures

- Use energy-efficient light bulbs.
- Turn off lights, televisions, videos, stereos, computers when you don't need them.
- Use the washing machine or dish washer only when they are full.
- When taking a shower, don't stand under the shower for hours.
- Turn off the engine when waiting in your car.

Home energy survey

Question	Yes	No	Tips – to save your family money and reduce your CO_2 emissions
Are there any drafts around your home's windows and doors?		X	By draft excluding you could save money on your heating bill.
Are there any curtains or furniture in front of your radiators?		X	Anything in front of your radiators will block the heat.
When you are cold, do you turn up the heating?		X	Save money by putting a jumper on.
Does your home have a programmable thermostat?	X		Turn the room temperature down by one degree centigrade. This can save up to £ 30 a year.
Are your home's walls insulated?	X		Insulation in your walls helps to keep your heat in, the cold out and will save you money on your heating bill.
Do you leave lights and electrical appliances on when they're not in use?		X	Leaving lights on in rooms that are not being used is a waste of energy and costs you money on your bill.
Do you have any low energy light bulbs in your home?	X		Low energy or energy efficient light bulbs produce less waste heat and last up to ten times longer than ordinary bulbs.
Do you leave electrical appliances on standby?		X	Switch appliances off properly as they use energy even on standby. 85 per cent of the energy used by a DVD is wasted when it is not in use. Saves up to £ 11 a year.
Do any of your electrical appliances have an energy efficiency logo?	X		A rating is the best – look at the Energy Savings Trust website for more details.
Are your clothes washed on a hot cycle?		X	Wash laundry loads on the low-temperature programme to save energy that would heat the water.
Is a tumble dryer used to dry your clothes?		X	In summer dry your clothes outside or if you have to use a tumble dryer, don't put really wet clothes inside.
Is a microwave oven used to cook small amounts of food?	X		Microwaves save money because you don't waste energy heating containers or air – as is the case in half-empty ovens.
Do you use lids on your saucepans when cooking your food?	X		Put a lid on saucepans, so the contents heat quicker and you use less energy.
Do you recycle in your home?	X		Recycling not only cuts down on the amount of waste going to landfill, it helps to reduce the amount of energy that would be used to make new products from raw materials.
Do you have a bath rather than a shower?		X	An ordinary shower uses only two-fifths of the water needed for a bath. Power showers use as much as a bath, and sometimes even more.
Do you have more than one car?		X	Cars produce more emissions than taking the bus, tram, train or walking or cycling.

"Home energy survey": Friends of the Earth, *Shout about climate change*, p. 15

How to launch an information campaign

Strategy Sheet **27**

To launch an information campaign you need to think about the following questions:

1. What is the aim of your information campaign?

2. What is your target group?

3. What information do you want to present?
Depending on your aim and your target group you should choose and structure the information you are going to present.

4. How do you want to present the information?
There are a lot of different ways of presenting information:
- You can arrange all available materials on posters and exhibit them on walls or on boards.
- You can design a leaflet.
- You can produce a film.
- You can write and act out a theatre play.
- You can give a public talk.

5. Where do you want to present the information?
You can e.g. present the information in a classroom, in the school hall, outside school.

6. When do you want to present the information?
You can e.g. present the information as a permanent exhibition, during lessons, during breaks, after school.

✂ -

Worksheet **28**

A piece of art created by Fides Maria Sigeneger for the project "Visual energy. Nach Tschernobyl – Ressourcen, Energien und wir" carried out by the Academy for Design and Art Charkiw and the Kunsthochschule Berlin-Weißensee.

Review

1. Bring along all the pictures you have collected during the last weeks that have anything to do with the topic "global warming" (see Getting started, p. 6, Nr. 4). Spread them out on the floor. Choose one or two pictures – not necessarily your own. With what you have learnt about global warming in mind describe them, comment on them and pin them to the wall or to the board, arranging and organizing them, thereby creating a collage covering the different aspects of "global warming":

- Effects of global warming
- A definition of global warming
- Solutions to global warming

2. Remember all the questions you have written down on a poster concerning the topic of "global warming" (see Getting started, p. 6, Nr. 3). Go through the questions again and make sure all your questions have been answered during the previous lessons. If not, try to find the answers.

3. Here are some of today's newspaper headlines concerning global warming:

World's Climate on Thin Ice

Water, Water, Everywhere

Warming Threatens Ocean Wildlife

Climate Scientists Issue Dire Warning

Alternative Energy Still Awaits Its Day

Climate Change Impact Disputed

End of the World Nigh – It's Official

First, discuss the headlines. Then, create headlines for newspaper articles to be printed in 20 years time. Compare today's headlines with those of the future.
Develop your headlines into newspaper reports.
Here are some questions to take into consideration:

- What effects has global warming caused so far?
- Has global warming been stopped, or have the effects become even worse? If so, why?
- What could have been done and what could be done to combat global warming?

4. The well-known American writer Ernest Callenbach, who is very concerned about environmental issues in general, has come up with a list of rules for mankind to follow in order to protect the earth, called "Earth's Ten Commandments". In your opinion, which rules should mankind obey to protect the earth?
Now, write down your own "Earth's Ten Commandments", starting with
Thou shalt … / Thou shalt not …
Read Callenbach's Earth's Ten Commandments. Explain and discuss them.

Ernest Callenbach, Earth's ten commandments

Thou shalt love and honor the Earth for it blesses thy life and governs thy survival.

Thou shalt keep each day sacred to the Earth and celebrate the turning of its seasons.

Thou shalt not hold thyself above other living things nor drive them to extinction.

Thou shalt give thanks for thy food to the creatures and plants that nourish thee.

Thou shalt limit thy offspring for multitudes of people are a burden unto the Earth.

Thou shalt not kill nor waste Earth's riches upon weapons of war.

Thou shalt not pursue profit at the Earth's expense but strive to restore its damaged majesty.

Thou shalt not hide from thyself or others the consequences of thy actions upon the Earth.

Thou shalt not steal from future generations by impoverishing or poisoning the Earth.

Thou shalt consume material goods in moderation so all may share Earth's bounty.

www.ernestcallenbach.com/earth.htm

Klausur 1

Mark Lynas

Six degrees

One day, 251 million years ago, a giant volcanic eruption shook modern-day Siberia. Billions of tonnes of hot ash and gases poured into the atmosphere, sparking huge storms of acid rain. Once the clouds cleared, the sun shone hotter than ever before, and searing heat killed plants and animals where they stood all around the planet. The end-Permian mass extinction had begun.
It was the worst ever crisis to affect life on Earth, and by the end up to 95% of the world's species were dead. In the words of one expert, it was the time 'when life nearly died'. Geologists examining the strata of rocks spanning the Permian Triassic boundary were stunned to see an abundance of fossils suddenly giving way to monotonous black mudstone – a telltale sign of anoxia, the crippling shortage of oxygen, as billions of lifeless bodies decayed at the bottom of the sea, having washed down from the ravaged land masses.
The crisis wasn't caused by an asteroid, unlike the catastrophe that later wiped out the dinosaurs. It was caused by global warming. The Siberian volcanoes had released vast quantities of carbon dioxide from deep within the Earth's crust, thus warming the climate sufficiently for massive amounts of methane to 'burp' out of the ocean, triggering a runaway greenhouse effect.
Life in this 'post-apocalyptic greenhouse' was so severe that only one large land animal survived – the adaptable piglike Lystrosaurus, which became the ancestor of the dinosaurs. It took another fifty million years for pre-extinction levels of biodiversity to return.
Geologists examining oxygen isotopes in the end-Permian rocks have recently put a figure on how much global warming was associated with this catastrophic mass extinction. That figure is six degrees Celsius.
Skip forwards 251 million years to the present day. The world is warming fast, and the evidence is everywhere, from thawing glaciers to rising sea levels. In 2001 the IPCC released its landmark Third Assessment Report, which made projections for future warming over the next hundred years.
The upper limit was higher than in previous assessments.
The scientists had raised it – to six degrees.

Mark Lynas: High Tide – News from a warming world, Hammersmith, London, Flamingo, 2004, pp. 299f.

searing burning

stratum a layer or set of layers of rock, earth
to span to last all through a period of time
abundance a large quantity that is more than enough
ravaged devastated

to thaw to melt
IPCC Intergovernmental Panel on Climate Change

1. Write a summary of the text in not more than 150 words. *20 credits*

2. What – to your mind – are the writer's intentions? Explain. *10 credits*

3. What can be done to prevent the catastrophe Lynas forecasts from happening? *20 credits*

4. "There is no bigger problem than climate change. The threat is quite simple, it's a threat to our civilization." (David A. King, Chief Scientific Advisor to the British Government, June 2004) Discuss King's statement. *30 credits*

Total: 80 credits

Klausur 1: Erwartungshorizont

1. Summary

At the end of the Permian era (251 million years ago) massive volcanic eruptions in present-day Siberia caused catastrophic changes in climate, which eventually resulted in the unequalled extinction of 95 % of the world's species. Huge releases of CO_2 from the Siberian volcanoes triggered off a warming of the climate causing methane to "burp" out of the oceans in enormous quantities. This led to a runaway greenhouse effect. Only fifty million years later did biodiversity regain its pre-extinction level. Recently scientists have found out that a temperature rise of six degrees Celsius was responsible for this end-Permian mass extinction. This is the same temperature rise scientists predict for the future warming of today's world over the next hundred years.

2. The writer's intentions

Lynas wants

- the reader to become aware of the serious threat of climate change by providing evidence of similar events in the past;
- to appeal to the reader to take action to combat global warming by stressing the dramatic consequences a temperature rise of six degrees Celsius would have for any life on earth.

3. Measures to be taken to prevent the catastrophe Lynas forecasts from happening

The overall aim is to reduce greenhouse gas emissions by for example

- promoting renewable energy production;
- promoting nuclear power;
- storing carbon underground (carbon sequestration);
- trading of carbon emissions;
- taking personal action, e.g. saving energy at home, using hybrid cars.

4. Discussion – possible points

Agreeing with King's statement:

- There is no denying that climate change is in full progress: rising temperatures, melting polar caps, receding glaciers, increased flooding, heavy storms, etc.
- Obviously the environment is collapsing with devastating impacts on human societies and terrestrial eco-systems all around the world, for example island nations are inundated by rising tides, coastal areas are devastated by violent storms (e.g. Katrina), melting permafrost damages Alaskan houses, bridges and roads.
- Climate change might already be at the tipping point.
- Time is running out for the world to stop global warming. Urgent action is needed.
- The question whether the earth can be saved has to remain unanswered as mankind is facing an unpredictable Mother Nature.
- There are other global problems like terrorism, diseases, poverty, etc. but they don't threaten mankind as such and as much.

Disagreeing with King's statement:

- There is no substantial evidence that climate change is underway to an extent that life on earth is threatened.
- Man will find solutions to stop climate change, for example the banning of CFCs (chlorofluorcarbons) seems to be leading to a closing-up of the ozone hole.
- Other global problems like terrorism or global diseases can have a similar devastating effect.

Klausur 2

George Monbiot

The struggle against ourselves

Speech to the Climate March, 3rd December 2005

I want to take a moment to remind you of where we have come from.

For the first three million years of human history, we lived according to circumstance. Our lives were ruled by the happenstances of ecology. We existed, as all animals do, in fear of hunger, predation, weather and disease.

For the following few thousand years, after we had grasped the rudiments of agriculture and crop storage, we enjoyed greater food security, and soon destroyed most of our non-human predators. But our lives were ruled by the sword, the axe and the spear. The primary struggle was for land. We needed it not just to grow our crops but also to provide our sources of energy – grazing for our horses and bullocks, wood for our fires.

Then we discovered fossil fuels, and everything changed. No longer were we constrained by the need to live on ambient energy; we could support ourselves by means of the sunlight stored over the preceding 350 million years. The new sources of energy permitted the economy to grow – to grow sufficiently to absorb some of the people expelled by the previous era's land disputes. Fossil fuels allowed both industry and cities to expand, which permitted the workers to organise and to force the despots to loosen their grip on power.

Fossil fuels helped us fight wars of a horror never contemplated before, but they also reduced the need for war. For the first time in human history, indeed for the first time in biological history, there was a surplus of available energy. We could keep body and soul together without having to fight someone else for the energy we needed. Agricultural productivity rose 10 or 20 fold. Economic productivity rose 100 fold. Most of us could live as no one had ever lived before.

And everything you see around you results from that. We have been able to assemble here from all corners of the country because of fossil fuels. We have not been charged and cut down by the yeomanry – or not yet at any rate – because of fossil fuels. Our freedoms, our comforts, our prosperity are all the result of fossil fuels.

Ours are the most fortunate generations that have ever lived. Ours are the most fortunate generations that ever will. We inhabit the brief historical interlude between ecological constraint and ecological catastrophe.

I don't have to remind you of the two forces which are converging on our lives. We are faced with an impending shortage of the source of energy which is hardest to replace – liquid fossil fuels. And we are faced with the environmental consequences of the fossil fuel burning which has permitted us to be standing here now. The structure, the complexity, the diversity of our lives, everything we know, everything that we have taken for granted, that looked solid and non-negotiable, suddenly looks contingent. All this is a great tottering pile balanced on a ball, a ball that is about to start rolling downhill.

I hear people talking about the carbon cuts they would like to see. I am not interested in what people would like to see. I am interested in what the science says. And the science is clear. We need not a 20% cut by 2020; not a 60% cut by 2050, but a 90% cut by 2030. Only then do we stand a good chance of keeping carbon concentrations in the atmosphere below 430 parts per million, which

happenstance *Zufall*
predation the act of an animal killing and eating other animals
rudiments basics

to be constrained to be restricted
ambient *umgebend*

yeomanry farmers who became soldiers

impending that is going to happen soon

non-negotiable sth that cannot be discussed
contingent to depend on sth
tottering unsteady, shaky

means that only then do we stand a good chance of preventing some of the threatened positive feedbacks. If we let it get beyond that point there is nothing we can do. The biosphere takes over as the primary source of carbon. It is out of our hands.

The notion that we can achieve this by replacing fossil fuels with ambient energy is a fantasy. It is true that we have untapped sources of energy in wind, waves, tides and sunlight, but it is neither so concentrated nor so consistent that we can plug it in and carry on as before.

A cut like this requires massive reductions in our energy use. There are some technofixes available, but they are unlikely to take us more than halfway there. If carbon emissions are to be capped at 10 %, energy use will have to be capped at under 50 %. The only fair means of doing this is national rationing accompanied by global contraction and convergence.

And we find ourselves in an extraordinary position. This is the first mass political movement to demand less, not more. The first to take to the streets in pursuit of austerity. The first to demand that our luxuries, even our comforts, are curtailed.

These are the greatest political challenges any movement has faced. But we are rising to it. We are rising. But let no one tell you it will be easy. If it were just a matter of slagging off George Bush, we would have won by now. But we must struggle not only against him, not only against our own government, not only against each other, but also against ourselves. The struggle against climate change is a struggle against much of what we have become. It is a struggle against some of our most fundamental urges.

We cannot call on others to stop flying if we still fly. We cannot ask the government to force us to change if we are not ready to change. The greatest fight of our lives will be fought not just out there, but also in here.

www.monbiot.com/archives/2005/12/05/the-struggle-against-ourselves

untapped available but not yet used

to be capped to be limited

contraction the process of becoming smaller

austerity *Enthaltung*
to curtail to limit

to slag off to say critical things about sb

1. What, in Monbiot's view, is the role of fossil fuels in human history? *10 credits*

2. With respect to the consumption of fossil fuels and its effects on the environment how does Monbiot view the present-day situation and what challenges does he see for the future? *10 credits*

3. Monbiot mentions wind, waves, tides and the sunlight as possible future sources of energy. What is his opinion of renewable energy? What do you think of renewable energy? Explain. *20 credits*

4. "Ours are the most fortunate generations that have ever lived. Ours are the most fortunate generations that ever will. We inhabit the brief historical interlude between ecological constraint and ecological catastrophe." (ll. 29–31) Explain and discuss. *20 credits*

Total: 60 credits

Klausur 2: Erwartungshorizont

1. The role of fossil fuels in human history

Fossil fuels

- represented new sources of energy;
- provided people with a surplus of available energy, freeing people from the constraints imposed by the need to live on ambient energy;
- led to cruel wars, but also reduced the need for war;
- allowed towns to expand;
- permitted the industry to expand;
- increased agricultural and particularly economic productivity;
- changed social systems, i.e. weakened the despots' power and strengthened the workers' power;
- gave and still gives people freedom;
- has raised people's living standards;
- enabled and continues to enable people to live in prosperity.

2. Fossil fuels consumption and its effects on the environment

The present-day situation:

- People are faced with an impending shortage of fossil fuels, which are very hard to replace.
- People are confronted with the environmental consequences of the burning of fossil fuels.
- Nothing about today's life can be taken for granted anymore.
- The whole world, i.e. everything is about to change with people being unable to do anything about it.

The future:

- A 90% cut by 2030 is needed if people want to prevent some of the threatened effects of global warming from happening.
- Energy use will have to be reduced by at least 50 %.
- Carbon emissions have to be cut not only nationally, but globally as well.
- Everybody will have to change his/her lifestyle, i.e. give up some of his/her luxuries and comforts.

3. Renewable energy seen by George Monbiot

Fossil fuels cannot be replaced by renewable energy, an energy source, which is unreliable, i.e. neither very concentrated nor consistent.

When answering this question, students can particularly refer to arguments discussed in Aspect 3, Task 3.

4. Explanation

Previous generations depended exclusively on the environment. Their lives were determined by hunger, weather, disease and the fear of being killed. Even if life improved with people learning how to farm the land and store crops and with people killing most of their non-human predators, previous generations still depended heavily on natural circumstances. Only when humankind discovered fossil fuels as an abundant source of energy did people's lives change for the better, i.e. for a life of freedom, comfort and prosperity. In contrast to our generations, who are enjoying this privileged life, the following generations will have to face the consequences of the extensive exploitation of fossil fuels as the main energy source of today's life: They will have to face global warming and its catastrophic effects on the environment.

Discussion – possible points

We are the most fortunate generations that have ever lived and that ever will, because

- we profit from the privileges brought about by the discovery of fossil fuels as the main source of energy, i.e. freedom, comfort, prosperity.
- people in future will have to tackle all the threatening effects of global warming:
  - melting of poles,
  - rising sea levels,
  - extinction of species,

– increase in human diseases,
– more extreme weather, e.g. hurricanes,
– etc.

We are not the most fortunate generations that have ever lived and that will ever live, because

- not everyone has access to fossil fuels, which has led and will lead to a growing gap between rich and poor.
- terrible and cruel wars have recently been fought and are still being fought over fossil fuels.
- future generations will improve the already known technologies or invent new technologies to generate alternative energy and to cope with global warming.
- global warming is not real and will therefore not lead to an ecological catastrophe.

Bildnachweis

S. 6: © Andy Singer; S. 15: © 2004 Twentieth Century Fox; S. 22: Matthias Berghahn/Verlagsarchiv Schöningh; S. 24: entnommen aus: Laurence Pringle, Global Warming, The Threat of Earth's Changing Climate, New York, SeaStar Books, 2001, S. 11; S. 30: Eastpak; S. 36: entnommen aus: Guardian Weekly, January 20–26, 2006, S. 15; S. 38: Reinhild Kassing/Verlagsarchiv Schöningh; S. 41: Photo: Joe Klamar/Getty Images; S. 45: © Greenpeace; S. 53: Fides Maria Sigeneger

Challenges – Global learning in a globalised world

Modelle und Methoden für den Englischunterricht

Herausgegeben von Engelbert Thaler

America's Global Role – Leader or Loner?
Von Iris Edelbrock und Andrea Schulz
78 S., DIN A4, geh.
978-3-14-040206-4
in Vorbereitung

Global Conflicts – Political Solutions
Von Martin Kohn
54 S., DIN A4, geh.,
978-3-14-040203-3
9,80

Global Warming – Earth's Climate at the Tipping Point?
Von Katharina Einhoff
62 S., DIN A4, geh.
978-3-14-040201-9

The Changing Face of Multicultural Britain
Von Antje Blume
62 S., DIN A4, geh.
978-3-14-040202-6
in Vorbereitung

Popular Culture – Football, Films and Fashion
Von Engelbert Thaler
52 S., DIN A4, geh.
978-3-14-040211-8
9,80

Science (Fiction) in the Third Millennium
Von Kirsten Pottbäcker
62 S., DIN A4, geh.
978-3-14-040207-1
9,80

Terrorism – A Global Threat?
Von Patricia Anslinger und Gisa van Els
62 S., DIN A4, geh.
978-3-14-040200-2
9,80

Them and US – On the Way to One World?
Von Katrin Kollmeyer
62 S., DIN A4, geh.
978-3-14-040205-7
in Vorbereitung

Weitere Titel sind in Vorbereitung.

Fordern Sie unseren Prospekt zur kompletten Reihe an:
Informationen zum Nulltarif ✆ 08 00 / 1 81 87 87

SCHÖNINGH VERLAG
Postfach 2540 · 33055 Paderborn
Schöningh
E-Mail: info@schoeningh.de
Internet: www.schoeningh-schulbuch.de